ROCKIN' ROOT WORDS

Book 1: Grades 3–5

Book 1: Grades 3–5

ROCKIN' ROOT WORDS

Manisha Shelley Kaura and S. R. Kaura, M.D.
Illustrated by Zak Hamby

Prufrock Press Inc.
P.O. Box 8813
Waco, TX 76714-8813
Phone: (800) 998-2208
Fax: (800) 240-0333
http://www.prufrock.com

Dedication

To our respected parents and teachers, who make a difference.

Acknowledgements

We would love to assume all of the credit for this work; alas, this is not true. The work we have done, like any work, was built upon established knowledge. We owe debts of gratitude to Samuel Johnson, Noah Webster, the Oxford English Dictionary, Morrises, Robert Barnhart, and many other experts and researchers. We are also grateful for the countless teachers who work day and night to help children learn our marvelous mother tongue.

Many wonderful people have helped us—teachers, critics, and students. To name a few: Sheri Kozlowski, Cheryl King, our "gophers" Shawn and Sasha Kaura, Ms. Emily, Michaela Dew, and last and not least our volunteer project manager Monika Kaura (Manisha's Mom) who worked tirelessly to meet the deadline.

Several people were employed to move the manuscript from a chaos of word lists to a publishable product. Although they were paid for their service, we could never hope to pay them enough. We hope our heartfelt thanks will make up the difference. We want to thank Ms. Lacy Compton of Prufrock Press who made our life a lot easier by her skillful editing.

This daddy/daughter team put our heart and soul in the book you hold in your hands. We are grateful that you have picked it up and hope that you find it useful.

Very respectfully,
Manisha Shelley Kaura
S. R. Kaura

CONTENTS

INTRODUCTION

About This Book

We live in an age where we are totally bombarded by multimedia from all sides of our daily lives. Therefore, I wanted to create a tool that helped children learn while utilizing visual learning styles, so prevalent in our present day framework, namely our reliance on technology. The main purpose of the book series is to help children become better at managing information.

The largest part of this information comes to us in the form of the fundamental units of language which we refer to as "words." These words are not arbitrary solid blocks of letters put together but instead are made out of consistent word parts or chunks of letters. Here we will focus on the internal structure of the words, also known as "word parts" and "root words." The hope is to create independent word learners.

Although simple words like car are made out of small word parts, as taught in lower elementary schools, what we learn in higher education is that more complex academic words are made out of Greek and Latin word parts. A vast body of research has shown three compelling reasons for why every child should learn language using word parts. First, these word parts are scattered throughout our academic studies. Secondly, the human brain can easily capture word parts and retain them as patterns. Thirdly, after retention, patterns are stored systematically and permanently and can be recalled from memory for figuring out or decoding new words.

The seed for this book was planted when I was 9 years old, in the fourth grade. My Dad and I studied my sheet of vocabulary words sent home from school daily. While working on the homework, we talked more about actual words and would note that a large majority of the words appeared to have a consistent internal structure. We also noticed that some words had similar beginnings, endings, and guts. While researching the words more closely, we realized that the words did not just fall from the sky, but instead were constructed by someone who wanted the language to be more easily understood. Therefore, we further researched who, when, how, and why our language came to be.

As we pursued answers to all those questions, we studied dictionaries and etymology books; then Dad and I prepared multiple lists of the word parts and classified them into categories like prefixes, roots, and suffixes, and later divided them thematically into chapters. By making the lists, we wanted to construct a user-friendly manual in which our main goal was to introduce the complicated and esoteric field to children who do not possess significant knowledge of language study. The following paragraphs will elaborate further on the three compelling reasons mentioned before.

First of all, Greek and Latin word parts contribute to more than 60% of English, 70% to 90% of science terminology, 71% of social studies terminology, and a large part of mathematical terms (Farstrup & Samuels, 2008; Green, 1994). These roots are distinct and consistent to children learning the language. Students who learn Greek and Latin roots of the English language enjoy advantages such as comfort with big words, advanced awareness, and spelling improvement in science and technical language (Thompson, 2002). By studying these word parts, we will be able to understand the internal structure of words and learn word families, including those from other languages.

Secondly, the most compelling reason that we must learn using word parts is to see how scientifically the human brain functions as a pattern detector. We ultimately see patterns everywhere in nature, whether it is the wings of a butterfly, stripes on a zebra, or the color spectrum of a rainbow. In lower elementary grades this strategy has been used very successfully. When we analyze common words like car, it has an onset "c" and a rime "ar." Here you can use pattern "ar" and make words like tar, jar, bar, and so on. Another example pattern is "ook," used so one can learn words like cook, book, look, and took. Patterns like "ar" and "ook" are meaningless parts of a word, but nonetheless are very useful in building a large vocabulary in children.

As we move to upper elementary or middle school students, we encounter words with Greek and Latin roots, prefixes, and suffixes. Let us analyze the word "exit," which has two word parts, "ex," which means out and "it," which means to go. Therefore, we are able to recognize that an exit sign in a building tells you where to go out. The word atom is made from "a" which means no and "tom" which means cutting. The Greeks were brilliant, and without the help of an electron microscope, they still knew that if you kept on cutting any matter, then eventually you would not be able to cut it anymore and that smallest particle was labeled as an atom. Another example is reincarnation. Here logic is as useful as it is in math: re + in + carn + ation = again + into + body/flesh. When adding up the meanings to the word you can see that reincarnation means "a soul going back into the body or flesh again." You can probably see now that these are meaningful word parts that can be combined flexibly to make thousands of words. Therefore, learning the word parts is like a shortcut to mastering the English language. A benefit to such pattern learning is a higher level of comprehension with the context area text.

The third most compelling reason is the scientific-psycholinguistic process of storing and retrieving the words. We can input vocabulary in various ways. For example, if you learn one word at a time using rote memorization like denture (artificial teeth), dentist (tooth doctor), dental (pertaining to teeth), and dentine (part of a tooth), it will be stored in the brain separately lacking connections, just like free floating balloons as shown in Figure 1. Here words are free floating because they are not anchored at all. Suppose we tie these words together in a linear fashion using the root dent as the common feature (linking orthographically;

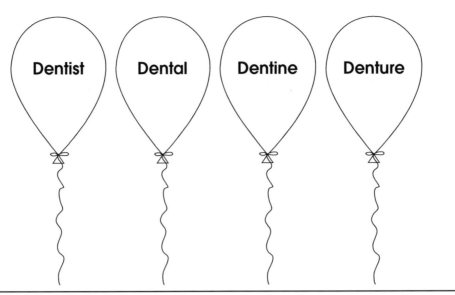

Figure 1. Individually learned words by rote memorization.

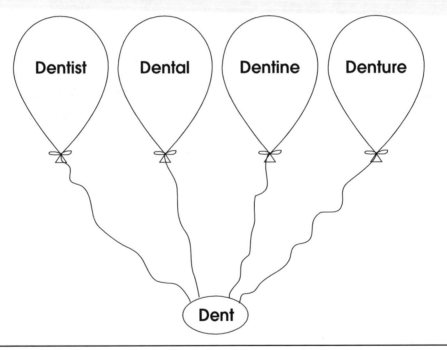

Figure 2. Orthographically-linked learned words.

see Figure 2). It will help children link the words together, and in return makes them easily retainable to memory. Still, this chain is only partially anchored in the brain. Later, more related words with the root "dent," like dentate, indentation, and indentured can be tied in and ultimately increase one's vocabulary.

Finally, we can take this process further by classifying these word parts thematically and memorizing them as concepts (see Figure 3).

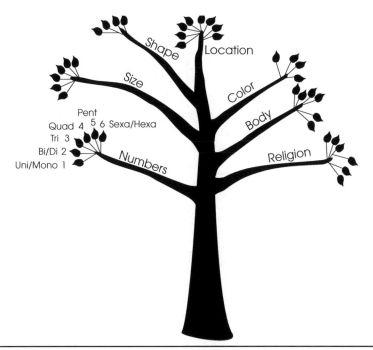

Figure 3. Thematically arranged as webs and root words learned as concepts.

We can tie the words together in visual webs to increase learning because we know visual memory contributes 70% to 90% of learning in humans. Such a strategy can improve reading comprehension, vocabulary, spelling, and word building. The brain learns not in a linear fashion, but instead in a highly interrelated web fashion so that information can be retrieved quickly.

How to Use This Book

This book displays word parts in three ways:
- Word beginnings—Greek and Latin prefixes, roots, and some combining forms and loan words;
- Word endings—Greek, Latin, and English suffixes used to make nouns, adjectives, verbs, and adverbs; and
- Root words—arranged thematically with some loan words and some combining forms.

The book is divided into 10 overview chapters based on various themes within our language. Within each chapter are lessons containing 5–10 words for children to learn, each based on one or more topic areas. For example, within the number chapter, students will encounter a lesson on words related to one hundred and one thousand.

Each of the lessons contains one or more word parts that define the lesson's content.

Each word part is presented in the following manner:

Sper comes from Latin signifying hope or expectation.

Beginning	Root Word	Ending	New Word	Definition
de	**sper**	ate	desperate	dangerously reckless or violent as from urgency

The new word part is given in italics, with an etymological note following it. This information is followed by at least one, but often many instances in which the word part is used in the construction of an English word (or sometimes a word borrowed from another language!). The word is presented in exploded form, to draw attention to the word part in question, then the word is represented in standard form. Finally, a definition appears on the right.

Many of the lessons contain web illustrations to help to show how one word part can help build words that span the language. For example, although "bio" means "life," it is not relegated to the life sciences. Several cartoons are scattered throughout the lessons to increase comprehension, and each lesson concludes with a brief activity to help students use their new knowledge. Finally, each chapter ends with a review activity to help children reinforce their learning.

We hope and believe that this program will impart a lasting understanding of the English language to all students, not just a familiarity with the words that we have the space to include.

CHAPTER I

Numbers

Numbering units can be as easy as the common 1, 2, 3, that we use every day or more complicated, such as the Roman numerals I, II, III. These numbers can even be represented with word prefixes, like uni-, di-, or tri- (which mean one, two, and three, respectively).

Numbers give a total count, amount, sum, or quantity. The word number comes from the Latin (through French)—*numerus*. We recognize a number as a digit, unit, quantity, or multitude. These combine with many prefixes and suffixes to create a number of words. By understanding and learning these prefixes and suffixes, one can understand several unfamiliar numerical words.

LESSON 1.1: NUMBER

Number comes from Latin and means total, sum, or one of a series or group. *Numer* also serves as a root for number.

Beginning	Root Word	Ending	New Word	Definition
	number	ed	numbered	counted
	numer	al	numeral	a figure or sign expressing a number
	numer	ous	numerous	many in number
	numer	ator	numerator	one who counts, or a number above the line in a fraction

MATCHING

Instructions: Match the words to their definitions.

Words
1. numbered
2. numeral
3. numerous
4. numerator

Definitions
a. someone who counts
b. many in number
c. symbol for a number
d. counted

FILL IN THE BLANK

Instructions: Use the words for Lesson 1.1 to complete the sentences below.

1. In order to take the spelling quiz, the teacher advised the class that the paper must be _____ from 1–10.

2. In math class we learned that the _____ is the number above the line in a fraction like ¾.

3. Because of my good grades in school my parents bought me _____ presents for my birthday.

4. II, III, IV and V are all symbols called Roman _____, that are used to describe numbers.

LESSON 1.2: ONE HALF AND ONE

ONE HALF

These prefixes let you know when something is halved. The Greek root for one-half is *hemi*, and the Latin prefixes are *semi* and *demi*. These roots also can make a word that means something has two parts or happens twice.

Beginning	Root Word	Ending	New Word	Definition
hemi	sphere	hemisphere	a half-sphere, as in the globe
hemi	circle	hemicircle	half-circle
semi	trailer	semi-trailer	type of freight trailer
semi	circle	semi-circle	a half circle

ONE

The prefixes *uni* (Latin) and *mono* (Greek) help determine when a word refers to only one of something, when parts are brought together, or when something applies to all parties.

Beginning	Root Word	Ending	New Word	Definition
uni	form	uniform	one form or shape
uni	corn	unicorn	a mythical animal having one horn
uni	cycle	unicycle	a vehicle with one wheel
mono	rail	monorail	form of transportation; electric trains running on one rail
mono	lith	monolith	one large carved stone, as found on Easter Island

WEB QUIZZES

Instructions: Try your hand at creating words! Connect the correct root word listed in the inner circle to the word parts listed in the outer circles. You may have to use a root word more than once!

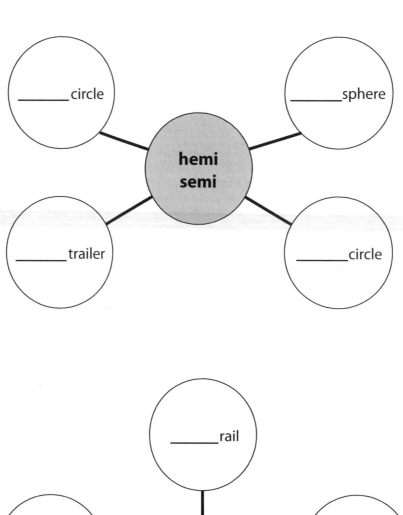

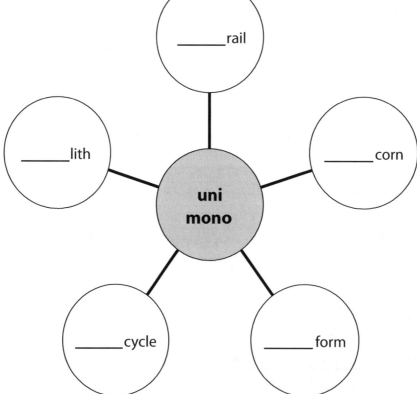

LESSON 1.3: TWO AND THREE

TWO

The prefixes *bi-* (Latin), *di-* (Greek), and *du-* signify two and can help you identify when something is made of or uses two significant parts, happens twice, or has two of something.

Beginning	Root Word	Ending	New Word	Definition
	bi	noculars	binoculars	long-distance magnifying device with two lenses
	bi	ped	biped	an animal that moves on two feet
	bi	focal	bifocal	having two points of focus; glasses
	di	oxide	dioxide	compound with two molecules of oxygen
	du	et	duet	short song sung by two people
	du	el	duel	combat between two persons

THREE

The prefix *tri-* comes from Latin and indicates when there is three of something. It is a common English prefix and often is an important clue to the meaning of a word.

Beginning	Root Word	Ending	New Word	Definition
	tri	ad	triad	a group of three people, things, or ideas
	tri	angular	triangular	having three angles and sides
	tri	pod	tripod	three-footed stand, as in a stool

THINKING ABOUT VOCABULARY

In old stories from England to Turkey, we hear of heroes having to complete three tasks. Three often is a number used in fairy tales (for example, "Goldilocks and the Three Bears"). We get three wishes. Is it mere coincidence?

Instructions: Use the vocabulary in this lesson to answer the following questions.

1. Name a fairy tale, other than "Goldilocks and the Three Bears," a nursery rhyme, or another fictional story that includes three of something.

   _____

2. When taking a group picture, what would be a useful tool to set your camera on?

   _____

3. If you could have three wishes, what would they be? (You cannot wish for more wishes!)

   _____

   _____

WEB QUIZ

Instructions: Try your hand at creating words! Connect the correct root word listed in the inner circle to the word parts listed in the outer circles. You may have to use a root word more than once!

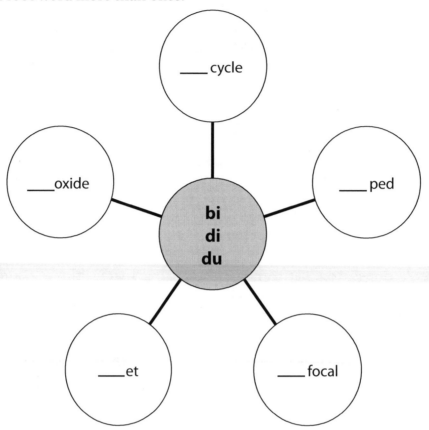

Rockin' Root Words Book 1 © Prufrock Press Inc. • Permission is granted to photocopy or reproduce this page for single classroom use only.

Lesson 1.4: Four and Five

FOUR

The roots for the number four are *quadr* (Latin), *quart*, and *tetra* (Greek).

Beginning	Root Word	Ending	New Word	Definition
	quadr	angle	quadrangle	a plane figure with four angles and four sides
	quadr	uplets	quadruplets	four babies born to the same mother at the same time
	tetra	pod	tetrapod	an animal with four legs or limbs
	quart	er	quarter	one fourth of a whole
	quart	et	quartet	a musical ensemble of four players

FIVE

The prefix for five is *pent* or *penta*, which comes from Greek. These handy prefixes tell you when a word's meaning contains or describes five of something.

Beginning	Root Word	Ending	New Word	Definition
	penta	gon	pentagon	a closed shape with five sides and angles; a U.S. military complex in Arlington, VA
	pent	athlon	pentathlon	an ancient athletic contest consisting of five events: jumping, sprinting, discus-throwing, spear-throwing, and wrestling

MATCHING

Instructions: Match the root words to their definitions. Definitions can be used more than once.

Root Words
1. Quadr
2. Penta
3. Tetra
4. Quart

Definitions
a. four
b. five

FILL IN THE BLANK

Instructions: Use the words in the tables for Lesson 1.4 to complete the sentences below.

1. My mother delivered four babies at once called _____.

2. My grandfather gives me a _____ every time I clean my room.

3. A dog is a _____ because it has four legs.

4. My art teacher told me to draw a figure with five sides known as a

    _____.

LESSON 1.5: SIX, SEVEN, AND EIGHT

SIX

Hexa comes from Greek and Latin words for six and the prefix *sex* means six in Latin.

Beginning	Root Word	Ending	New Word	Definition
	hexa	gon	hexagon	a diagram with six sides and angles
	sex	tuplets	sextuplets	six babies born at the same time to one mother

SEVEN

The roots for seven are *sept*, which comes from Latin, and *hept*, which means seven in Greek. Both prefixes are used in English to describe when there are seven of something.

Beginning	Root Word	Ending	New Word	Definition
	sept	ember	September	seventh month of ancient Roman calendar
	sept	et	septet	group of seven musicians
	hept	agon	heptagon	figure with seven sides and angles
	hept	athlon	heptathlon	seven sports as part of one contest

EIGHT

Oct comes from the Greek for eight and describes one of the most unusual ocean dwellers, the octopus.

Beginning	Root Word	Ending	New Word	Definition
	oct	agon	octagon	a figure with eight sides and angles
	oct	ave	octave	eighth day after a festival, or eight notes above in music
	oct	ober	October	eighth month of the ancient Roman calendar

Rockin' Root Words Book 1 © Prufrock Press Inc. • Permission is granted to photocopy or reproduce this page for single classroom use only.

MORE OR LESS?

Instructions: Look at the sets of words below and choose whether the first word in each set is more or less than the other.

1. **oct** (more than, less than) **hexa**

2. **sex** (more than, less than) **sept**

3. **hept** (more than, less than) **oct**

WEB QUIZ

Instructions: Try your hand at creating words! Connect the correct root word listed in the inner circle to the word parts listed in the outer circles. You may have to use a root word more than once!

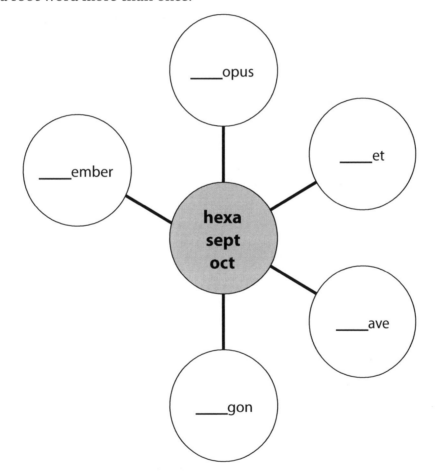

LESSON 1.6: NINE AND TEN

NINE

Non (Latin) means nine or the late stages or end of something.

Beginning	Root Word	Ending	New Word	Definition
	non	agon	nonagon	a figure with nine angles and sides
	non	et	nonet	a musical composition of nine voices or instruments
	non	agenarian	nonagenarian	a person at least 90 years old

TEN

Roots for the number 10 are *dec* for $\frac{1}{10}$ and *deca* for 10 times from Latin. These roots take many forms in English mathematical vocabulary.

Beginning	Root Word	Ending	New Word	Definition
	dec	imal	decimal	tenth part or one-tenth (.1)
	dec	imeter	decimeter	one-tenth of a meter
	dec	ade	decade	a period of 10 years
	dec	athlon	decathlon	a sporting event of 10 different sports
	deca	meter	decameter	ten meters

MAKE A WORD

Instructions: Match the correct root word and ending together to make five words. For example, the root word "non" and the ending "agon" together make the word "nonagon." The root words and endings can be used more than once.

Root Word	Ending	New Word
non	athlon	
dec	meter	
deca	agenarian	
	imeter	
	et	

FILL IN THE BLANK

Instructions: Use the words in the tables for Lesson 1.6 to complete the sentences below.

1. Every 10 years is considered to be a new _____.

2. When you have a remainder in math, you can write it as a _____.

3. A figure with nine sides is a _____.

LESSON 1.7: ONE HUNDRED AND ONE THOUSAND

ONE HUNDRED

Cent comes from Latin (through French) to mean one hundred of something.

Beginning	Root Word	Ending	New Word	Definition
	cent		cent	one one-hundredth ($\frac{1}{100}$) of a dollar
	cent	ury	century	one hundred years
	cent	ipede	centipede	a worm-like creature with numerous feet
	cent	imeter	centimeter	one one-hundredth ($\frac{1}{100}$) of a meter

ONE THOUSAND

Milli, from Latin by way of French, often is used in science, medicine, and industry to show one thousand of something or to indicate a part that is one thousandth of something. Similarly, *kilo* is used to mean one thousand and derives from Greek via French.

Beginning	Root Word	Ending	New Word	Definition
	milli	pede	millipede	a wormlike creature thought to have a thousand feet
	milli	meter	millimeter	one thousandth of a meter
	kilo	meter	kilometer	one thousand meters of distance
	kilo	gram	kilogram	one thousand grams (about 2.2 pounds)

MATCHING

Instructions: Match the root words to their definitions. Definitions can be used more than once.

Root Words
1. kilo
2. milli
3. cent

Definitions
a. one hundred
b. one thousand

ALL MIXED UP

Instructions: Help! The following word parts were all mixed up in the dictionary. Connect the word parts by drawing lines between the boxes. Then, write the correct words in the lines next to their definitions. Be careful! Some of the connections can be tricky: You only want to find words that match the definitions below.

1. _____ : one hundred years

2. _____ : one thousand meters

3. _____ : a creature thought to have one thousand feet

4. _____ : one one-hundredth (¹⁄₁₀₀) of a meter

5. _____ : one thousand grams

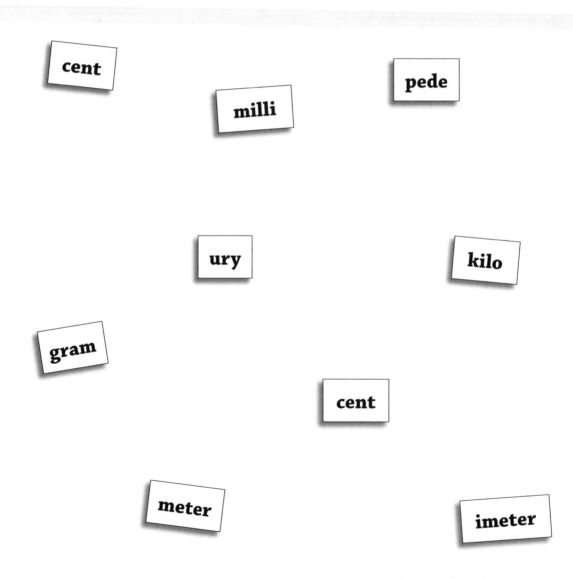

cent

milli

pede

ury

kilo

gram

cent

meter

imeter

LESSON 1.8: FIRST AND LAST

FIRST

Prim (Latin), *proto* (Greek), and *arch* (French, Latin, and Greek) indicate something as first in a sequence, the main focus, or the leader of a project or group.

Beginning	Root Word	Ending	New Word	Definition
	prim	ary	primary	first in rank, chief, main
	prim	ate	primate	a mammal, such as a monkey or ape
	proto	zoa	protozoa	first animals; microscopic creatures
	prot(o)	agonist	protagonist	the principal character in a literary work
	proto	type	prototype	a first impression or model
	arch	ives	archives	a place where old records are kept
	arch	itect	architect	first or chief builder or designer

LAST

Ulti comes from Latin.

Beginning	Root Word	Ending	New Word	Definition
	ulti	mate	ultimate	last or final in a series
	ulti	matum	ultimatum	final condition, stipulation, or demand

WHAT DOESN'T BELONG?

Instructions: Choose the word in each line that *does not* mean the same as the first word.

1. **ultimate**   last   final   first

2. **primary**   first   secondary   chief

3. **primate**   reptile   mammal   monkey

4. **prototype**   first impression   finished product   model

5. **ultimatum** final demand   final draft   final condition

FILL IN THE BLANK

Instructions: Use the words in the tables for Lesson 1.8 to complete the sentences below.

1. My mom gave me an _____ to either do the dishes or go to my room.

2. A monkey is considered to be the first mammal known as a _____.

3. In the library we have a large amount of _____ on the 19th century.

4. I created a rough drawing or _____ of my invention project before

   building my final version.

CHAPTER I REVIEW

WORD BUBBLES

Instructions: Add the prefixes in the word bank to the bubbles to make words that match the definitions.

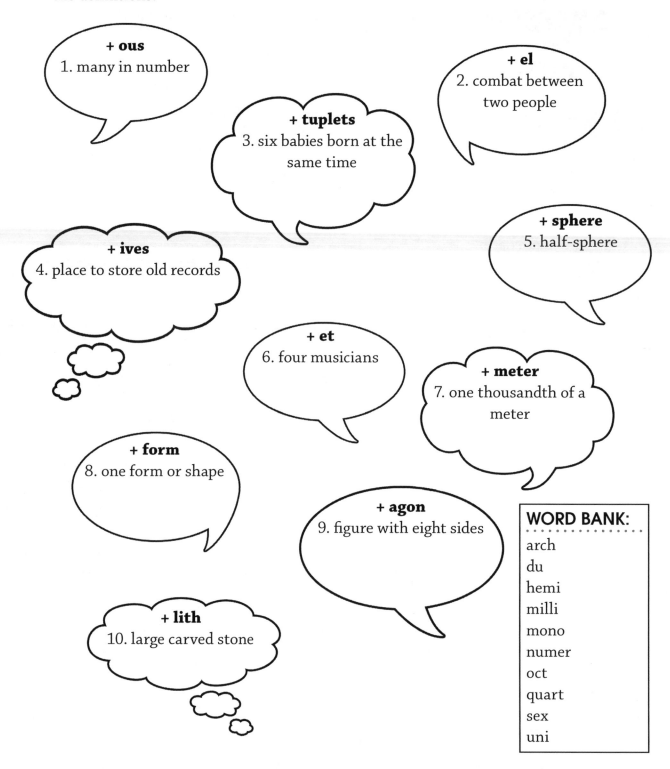

+ ous
1. many in number

+ el
2. combat between two people

+ tuplets
3. six babies born at the same time

+ ives
4. place to store old records

+ sphere
5. half-sphere

+ et
6. four musicians

+ meter
7. one thousandth of a meter

+ form
8. one form or shape

+ agon
9. figure with eight sides

+ lith
10. large carved stone

WORD BANK:
arch
du
hemi
milli
mono
numer
oct
quart
sex
uni

CHAPTER 2

Quantifiers and Size

Aside from our sense of good, bad, and neutral, nothing shapes the ways we look at the world around us more than our sense of quantity. From the time we are babies, quantity words fall into three general categories: none, one, and some. Many quantity words will be familiar to you as a result.

We also cover words dealing with size in this chapter. As we know, people tend to exaggerate, so naturally our language has a great number of words to describe the relative largeness or smallness of objects. Many of these words have been pulled from Latin and Greek.

LESSON 2.1: EQUAL AND BOTH

EQUAL

The prefixes for equality are *iso*, from Greek, and *equa/equi*, from Latin. These prefixes have many uses in mathematical language and can help you understand meanings of equality and sameness.

Beginning	Root Word	Ending	New Word	Definition
iso	metric	isometric	equal measurement
iso	sceles	isosceles	equal legs of a triangle
equa	l	equal	of the same size, quantity, or number
equa	tor	equator	imaginary line around the middle of the globe
equi	lateral	equilateral	a triangle with sides of equal measurement

BOTH

Knowing the prefixes *amph* and *amphi*, from Greek, can help you decipher words with meanings like both or surrounding.

Beginning	Root Word	Ending	New Word	Definition
amph(i)	bian	amphibian	animals that can live in both water and on land
amph(i)	theater	amphitheater	a theater in which the seats surround the stage
amph(i)	ora	amphora	a jar with two handles, one on each side

WORD SPLITS

Instructions: The makers of a new dictionary want to break up some words into their word parts for their new edition, but need your help! Can you divide the following words into their word parts? Think carefully—a few words may be new to you!

1. amphitheater: _____ + _____

2. isometric: _____ + _____

3. equal: _____ + _____

4. equation: _____ + _____

5. isotope: _____ + _____

MAKE A WORD

Instructions: Match the correct root word and ending together to make six words. For example, the root word "non" and the ending "agon" together make the new word "nonagon." The root words and endings can be used more than once.

Root Word	Ending	New Word
iso	ora	
equa	tor	
equi	sceles	
amph(i)	bian	
	lateral	
	nox	

LESSON 2.2: MANY AND ALL/FULL

MANY

The prefixes for "many" are *plu and plur* from Latin (through French), *multi* (from Latin), and *poly* (from Greek). These prefixes clue when a word's meaning refers to gain, an increase, or more than one.

Beginning	Root Word	Ending	New Word	Definition
	plu	s	plus	addition, gain
	plur	al	plural	more than one
	multi	ply	multiply	to cause to increase in numbers
	multi	plex	multiplex	a movie theater with many screens
	poly	gon	polygon	a shape with many angles

ALL/FULL

The prefixes for all and full are *cop* (Latin), *pan* (Greek), and *holo* (Greek, through Latin and French). These prefixes tell you that a word deals with a large amount, an abundance, or a wholeness.

Beginning	Root Word	Ending	New Word	Definition
	cop	ious	copious	very plentiful, abundant
cornu	**cop**	ia	cornucopia	horn of plenty, an overflowing fullness
	pan	orama	panorama	complete all-around view of a scene
	holo	gram	hologram	three-dimensional illusion
	holo	caust	Holocaust	a whole, burnt offering; the mass destruction of European Jews during World War II

CHANGE IT UP

Instructions: Replace the underlined word or words in each sentence with one of the vocabulary words in the word bank.

Word Bank: plural, panoramic, copious, multiplied, Holocaust, plus, polygons

1. My teacher taught me that one <u>added to</u> one equals two.
2. When my dad got 10 new cows, his herd <u>increased in numbers.</u>
3. In history class we learned about the <u>mass destruction of European Jews</u> that occurred in World War II.
4. I have a plentiful and <u>abundant</u> amount of money in my piggy bank.
5. By standing at the mountain's lookout we had a <u>complete and all-around</u> view of the valley below.
6. She doodled during the lesson, drawing <u>figures with many sides</u> on her paper.

WEB QUIZ

Instructions: Try your hand at creating words! Connect the correct root word listed in the inner circle to the word parts listed in the outer circles. You may have to use a root word more than once!

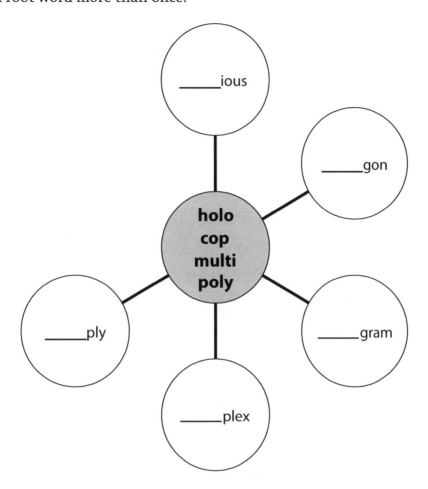

LESSON 2.3: SMALL

Min and *mini* come from the Italian word, *miniatura*. *Micro* comes from Greek and is commonly used in science. Both of these word roots pertain to small size or scale or to making less.

Beginning	Root Word	Ending	New Word	Definition
	min	us	minus	diminished in number or size by subtraction
di	**min**	ish	diminish	to make smaller
	mini	ature	miniature	something represented on a small scale
	mini	mum	minimum	the least quantity possible
	micro	scope	microscope	a device for making very small things look larger
	micro	phone	microphone	an instrument for magnifying and transmitting sounds

FILL IN THE BLANK

Instructions: Use the words for Lesson 2.3 to complete the sentences below.

1. As my grandmother got older, her hair started to _____ in thickness.

2. In science class, we looked at protozoa under a _____.

3. People always tell me that I am a _____ version of my older sister.

4. My brother always does the _____ amount of chores needed to be able to go outside.

5. By speaking into the _____, my tiny voice was made much louder, allowing the entire crowd to hear my speech.

WEB QUIZ

Instructions: Try your hand at creating words! Connect the correct root word listed in the inner circle to the word parts listed in the outer circles. You may have to use a root word more than once!

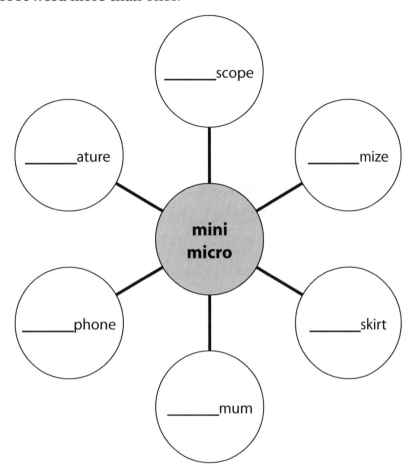

LESSON 2.4: LARGE

The roots *magn* (Latin) and *maxi* (Latin) indicate a word meaning largeness, greatness, or length.

Beginning	Root Word	Ending	New Word	Definition
	magn	ifier	magnifier	an object that makes things larger
	magn	ificent	magnificent	that which is great or wonderful
	magn	ate	magnate	a person of great importance and with lots of influence
	maxi	mum	maximum	great or large, largest or most possible or desirable
	maxi	mal	maximal	the upper limit
	maxi	mize	maximize	to make something the biggest or greatest it can be

THE GREAT DIVIDE

Instructions: Divide these words into two groups, placing similar words in each side of the Venn diagram using the definitions as a guide.

Word Bank: magnificent, maximize, magnate, maximum, magnify

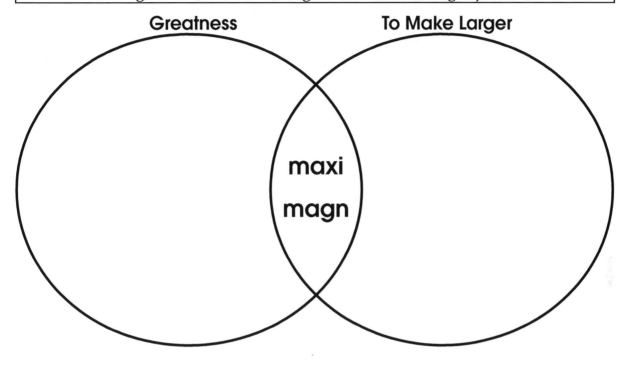

Greatness **To Make Larger**

maxi

magn

ADDING SUFFIXES

Instructions: The suffix "ize" means "to make." For example, maximize means to make something larger or greater. Minimize means to make something smaller. Using that knowledge, write a possible definition for each of the new words below.

1. realize

   _____

2. energize

   _____

3. legalize

   _____

4. visualize

   _____

5. summarize

   _____

LESSON 2.5: TALL/LONG AND SHORT/LOW

TALL/LONG

The roots for tall or long are *long*, *alti* (Latin), and *acro* (Greek). These roots find their way into many common English words and make up a number of science terms for length or height or for the arms and legs.

Beginning	Root Word	Ending	New Word	Definition
	long	itude	longitude	imaginary long lines from the North Pole to the South Pole that measure the distance east and west of the Prime Meridian
pro	long		prolong	to lengthen in time
	alti	meter	altimeter	instrument for measuring heights above ground or sea level
	alti	tude	altitude	elevation of an object
	acro	bat	acrobat	a performer of gymnastic tricks, sometimes high above the ground
	acro	nym	acronym	word made from first letters of different words that make a new word like SCUBA or self-contained underwater breathing apparatus

SHORT/LOW

Roots for short or low are *brev* (Latin, through French) and *bass/bas* (French). Knowing these roots helps you decide when a word pertains to a short amount of time, the shortening of an item, or a lowness of tone or situation.

Beginning	Root Word	Ending	New Word	Definition
	brev	ity	brevity	the quality of being of short duration or expressed in a few words
	bass	oon	bassoon	musical instrument that produces a deep, low sound
	bas	ement	basement	underground part of a building

MATCHING

Instructions: Match the root words to their definitions. Definitions can be used more than once.

Root Words
1. long
2. bas
3. bass
4. alti
5. brev
6. acro

Definitions
a. short/low
b. tall/long

FILL IN THE BLANK

Instructions: Use the words in the tables for Lesson 2.5 to complete the sentences below.

1. The airplane reached an _____ of 300,000 feet in the air.

2. We kept a lot of storage material in our home in the _____.

3. I tried out to play the _____ in the orchestra section of our school play.

4. The _____ at the circus was very athletic and flexible.

5. _____ is the north-south opposite of latitude.

6. A short speech is characterized by its _____.

CHAPTER 2 REVIEW

WORD JUMBLE

Instructions: Use the definitions below and your word tables in this chapter to fill in the blanks for each word. Then, unscramble the letters that appear in circles to find the answer to the jumbled word!

1. A shape with many sides is called a ◯ __ __ __ __ __ __.

2. Two or more things that are the same are said to be __ __ __ ◯ __.

3. The largest amount of something is the __ __ __ ◯ __ __ __.

4. When it comes to words, this is the opposite of singular. __ __ ◯ __ __ __

5. A __ __ __ __ ◯ __ __ __ __ is a term for a whole, burnt offering.

6. The smallest amount of something is the __ __ ◯ __ __ __ __.

7. Some actors perform in an open-air stadium called an
__ __ __ __ __ __ __ __ __ __ __ ◯.

8. A gymnast who performs high in the air is an __ __ __ ◯ __ __ __.

9. A __ __ __ __ __ ◯ __ is an instrument that produces a low, deep tone.

10. This is a triangle with two sides of equal lengths.
__ __ __ __ ◯ __ __ __ __

Jumbled Word: An overflowing fullness; an object to hold many items

__ __ __ __ __ __ __ __ __ __

Rockin' Root Words Book 1 © Prufrock Press Inc. • Permission is granted to photocopy or reproduce this page for single classroom use only.

CHAPTER 3

Time

Time is one of the most important factors in our lives. You have to wake up at a certain time to go to school. Recess is for a short time. At the conclusion of the school day, there is a time to go home and finish your homework. There are clocks everywhere. You cannot be late for school, just as your parents cannot be late for their jobs or appointments. Even early humans were aware of time—evidenced by inventions such as the astrolabe and sundial and concepts like day and night or the time from one full moon to the next. The first section of this chapter deals with words associated with periods of time. The second section deals with our measurement of time.

LESSON 3.1: TIME

The roots for time are *temp* and *tempor*, from Latin through French, and *chron/cron*, which comes to English from Greek and Latin. These roots give you a clue about when a word refers to the past, to time passing quickly, or to the sequence of time.

Beginning	Root Word	Ending	New Word	Definition
	temp	o	tempo	the rate of speed of a musical piece or motion
	tempor	ary	temporary	not permanent
	chron	icle	chronicle	historical events arranged in order of time
	chron	ology	chronology	the order of past events in sequence
	chron	ic	chronic	occurs for a long period of time

THINKING ABOUT VOCABULARY

Kronos was the Greek god of time, and he had a nasty habit of eating his children. His wife didn't like her children being treated this way, so she tricked Kronos by giving him a stone wrapped in a blanket, which he promptly ate. In doing so, she saved her son Zeus, who became the king of the gods and eventually destroyed Kronos.

Instructions: Answer the following questions about time.

1. Kronos was the Greek god of time. Name another myth, fable, or fairy tale in which time plays an important role in the story.

   _____

2. Something that is not permanent is said to be temporary. Based on your words above, something that is not temporary and lasts a long time can be called what?

   _____

3. Tempo is often used to determine the *pace* of music. What is another activity that requires you to keep up a tempo, or pace?

   _____

WEB QUIZ

Instructions: Try your hand at creating words! Connect the correct root word listed in the inner circle to the word parts listed in the outer circles. You may have to use a root word more than once!

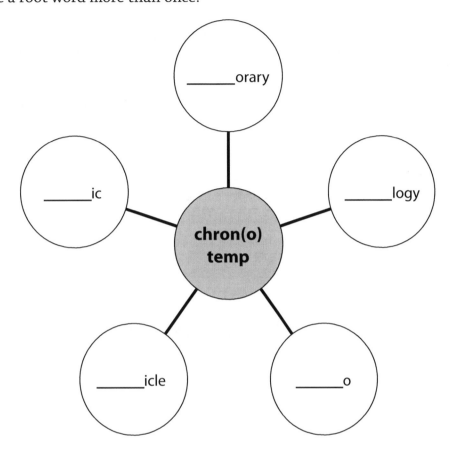

LESSON 3.2: BEFORE AND AFTER

BEFORE

Two prefixes help you decide when a word's meaning is *before* something else: *pre* and *ante* for before, in front of, or earlier. Both prefixes come from Latin.

Beginning	Root Word	Ending	New Word	Definition
pre	fix	prefix	a word part fixed in front of a root word that changes the meaning of its root
pre	dict	predict	to say beforehand, advise, or give notice
pre	caution	precaution	to guard against before things happen; a protective action
pre	mature	premature	before its time, early
ante	meridian	antemeridian	in the morning (A.M.)

AFTER

The prefixes for afterwards in time are *post* and *sec*.

Beginning	Root Word	Ending	New Word	Definition
post	war	postwar	after the war
post	meridian	postmeridian	in the afternoon (P.M.)
post	script	postscript	after writing a letter, an afterthought (p.s.)
sec	ond	second	comes after first in ordinal numbers
sec	ondary	secondary	comes after primary in numbers

FILL IN THE BLANK

Instructions: Use the words in the tables for Lesson 3.2 to complete the sentences below.

1. When the Civil War ended, American citizens had to deal with many

   _____ laws and regulations that dramatically changed society.

2. Some scientists _____ that global warming will cause the ice

   caps to melt.

3. My friend won a silver medal for her _____ place finish.

4. A.M. is an abbreviation for the word _____.

5. My little sister was born _____ so she had to stay in the

   hospital for 3 weeks.

WEB QUIZ

Instructions: Try your hand at creating words! Connect the correct root word listed in the inner circle to the word parts listed in the outer circles. You may have to use a root word more than once!

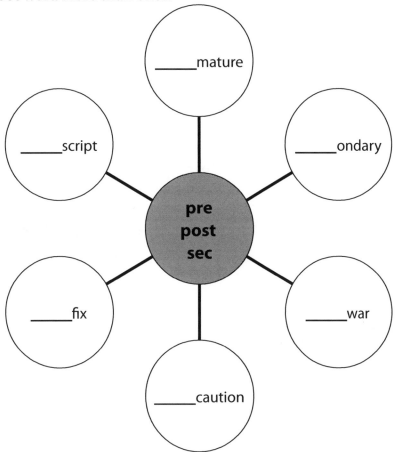

LESSON 3.3: Hour, Day, and Night

HOUR

Time was once measured with an hourglass and the root for hour, *hor*, is from Greek.

Beginning	Root Word	Ending	New Word	Definition
	hor	oscope	horoscope	a calendar of life events prepared and based on the hour of a child's birth and position of the stars at that time

DAY

The roots for day come from French as *jour*, and from Greek, through French and Latin, as *dia*, which takes on the additional meaning of passing through. This root also represents light and the passage of the day.

Beginning	Root Word	Ending	New Word	Definition
	dia	ry	diary	written record
	dia	l	dial	sundial, face of a clock
	journ	ey	journey	literally, a day's trip; now, any long trip
	journ	al	journal	a diary with daily entries
	journ	alism	journalism	the practice of writing mostly articles for newspapers or magazines

NIGHT

Noct comes from Latin through French and *nox* comes from Latin. *Nox* has the additional meanings of harm or injury or something offensive, as in obnoxious.

Beginning	Root Word	Ending	New Word	Definition
	noct	urnal	nocturnal	pertaining to nighttime
equi	**nox**		equinox	two days each year when the days and nights are of equal length

MATCHING

Instructions: Match the root words to their definitions. Definitions can be used more than once.

Root Words

1. nox
2. hor
3. dia
4. noct
5. jour

Definitions

a. hour
b. night
c. day

PICK THE WORD

Instructions: Circle the best word or phrase that completes each sentence.

1. When you write in a journal, you are keeping track of your life's events on a(n)

    (*infrequent, daily, yearly*) basis.

2. I think my dog must be nocturnal; he never wants to sleep at (*night,*

    daytime, dinnertime).

3. When I get older, I plan to take a long trip or a(n)

    (*quest, adventure, journey*) across North America.

4.   We got up extra early so that we could experience the start of this year's

    equinox, which is when day and night are of (*opposite, equal, shorter*)

    length.

LESSON 3.4: MONTH AND YEAR

LUNA-TICK

MONTH

Mon is the root for month or the time it takes for the moon to move from one full moon to the next. *Luna* comes from Latin through French and has an additional meaning of insanity.

Beginning	Root Word	Ending	New Word	Definition
	mon	day	Monday	day of the moon, from Old English
	mon	thly	monthly	occurring once a month
	mon	th	month	period of time between two full moons
	luna	r	lunar	of or belonging to the moon
	luna	tic	lunatic	one who suffers from madness; people once were thought to lose their minds due to a full moon

YEAR

The roots *ann* and *enn* come from Latin and indicate something that marks the year.

Beginning	Root Word	Ending	New Word	Definition
	ann	ual	annual	yearly
	ann	iversary	anniversary	a yearly marker of an event
per	**enn**	ial	perennial	present in all seasons of the year
cent	**enn**	ial	centennial	every 100 years

MAKE A WORD

Instructions: Match the correct root word and ending together to make seven words. For example, the root word "non" and the ending "agon" together make the new word "nonagon." The root words and endings can be used more than once.

Root Word	Ending	New Word
mon	atic	
lun	thly	
ann	iversary	
	day	
	ual	
	th	
	ar	

FILL IN THE BLANK

Instructions: Use the words for Lesson 3.4 to complete the sentences below.

1. Plants that live through all four seasons are known as _____.

2. My teacher said that we will have a test _____ until summer break.

3. My brother called the clown at the magic show a _____ because of all of his crazy tricks.

4. Allison's parents' celebrate their _____ in December.

5. This year celebrates my school's _____ or 100-year anniversary.

CHAPTER 3 REVIEW

THE WORD CLOCK

Instructions: Use the definitions on each section of the clock to help you fill in the missing words.

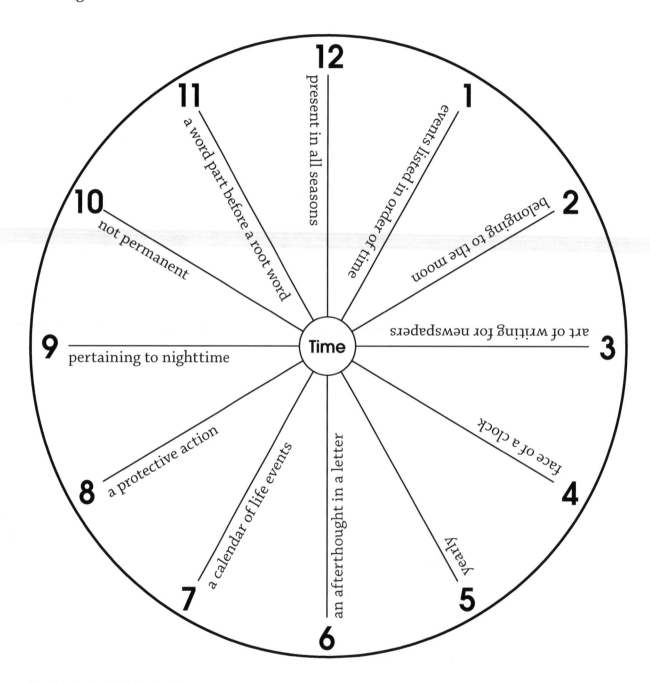

MY CHRONOLOGY

Instructions: Create a timeline of at least five of your life's events. First, draw a line. Then, place your events in chronological order along the timeline. Make sure to include the date! Some ideas for events to include are your birthday, your first day of school, and when your siblings were born.

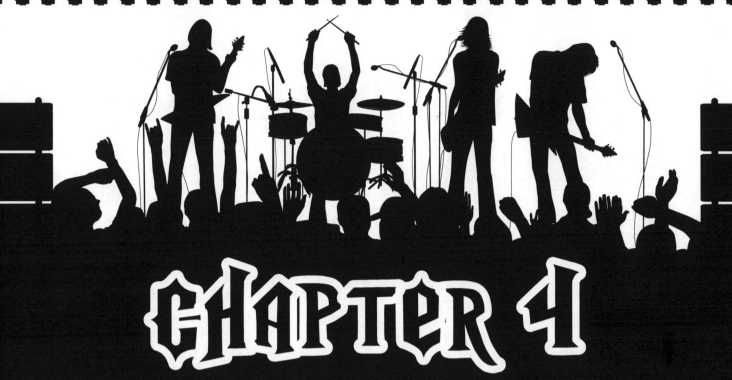

CHAPTER 4

Location, Directions, and Relationships

Good directions are helpful in finding a location, but what is a location? A location is where an object or person can be found and it is described with words such as up, ahead of, next to, or below. When you recognize and understand these words, you can find anything! Direction is simply the location of two objects, places, or people in relationship to each other. Directions guide us from one location to another.

LESSON 4.1: LOCATION

Top and *loc* are from Greek and Latin, respectively, and they help you know when a word's meaning has something to do with a place or spot or something unique. They also may describe a specific piece or part of something.

Beginning	Root Word	Ending	New Word	Definition
	top	ic	topic	matter written or spoken about
	top	iary	topiary	the art of trimming shrubs and bushes into fanciful shapes
u	**top**	ia	utopia	an ideal imaginary place
	loc	ation	location	place, spot, position
	loc	al	local	pertaining to a particular nearby place
	loc	omotive	locomotive	the engine of a railroad train
dis	**loc**	ate	dislocate	to force out of place
al	**loc**	ate	allocate	to set aside a portion of a budget for a particular purpose

WORD SPLITS

Instructions: The makers of a new dictionary want to break up some words into their word parts for their new edition, but need your help! Can you divide the following words into their word parts? Think carefully—a few words may be new to you!

1. location: _____ + _____

2. allocate: _____ + _____ + _____

3. topography: _____ + _____

4. dislocate: _____ + _____ + _____

5. relocate: _____ + _____ + _____

6. utopia: _____ + _____ + _____

WEB QUIZ

Instructions: Try your hand at creating words! Connect the correct root word listed in the inner circle to the word parts listed in the outer circles. You may have to use a root word more than once!

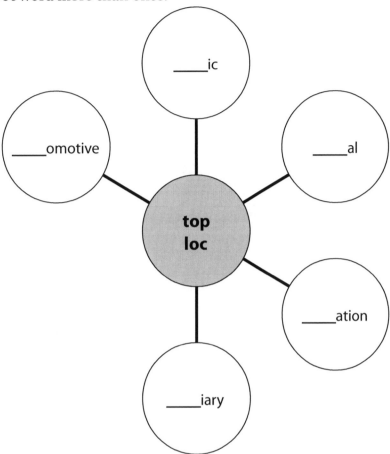

LESSON 4.2: ABOVE

ABOVE

The combining forms are *epi* (Greek), *super* (Latin), *over,* and *out* (Middle English). These roots offer clues about words referring to being on something, completeness, excessiveness, or being beyond or more than what is normal.

Beginning	Root Word	Ending	New Word	Definition
epi	center	epicenter	Earth surface directly above the origin of an earthquake
epi	taph	epitaph	inscription on a tombstone
epi	sode	episode	a complete scene in a literary work
super	ficial	superficial	on the surface only
super	visor	supervisor	manager, director, overseer
super	market	supermarket	large grocery store
over	alls	overalls	denim, bibbed pants
over	flow	overflow	when a liquid exceeds its container, or any extra that cannot be contained or managed
out	law	outlaw	habitual criminal; someone "beyond the law"
out	let	outlet	mouth of a river; a store that sells goods of a specific manufacturer

SYNONYM SEARCH

Instructions: Sort through the words in the word bank to find synonyms for the vocabulary words listed below. Write the synonyms on the lines next to the words they correspond with. Be careful—some of the words in the word bank will not be used!

> **Word Bank:** extra, scene, surface, manager, grocery store, inscription, criminal, river mouth, pants

1. supervisor

   _____

2. overflow

   _____

3. epitaph

   _____

4. outlaw

   _____

5. superficial

   _____

WEB QUIZ

Instructions: Try your hand at creating words! Connect the correct root word listed in the inner circle to the word parts listed in the outer circles. You may have to use a root word more than once!

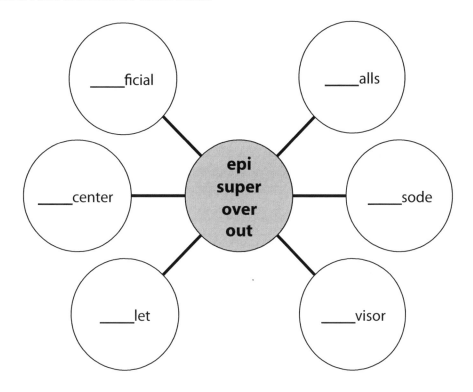

LESSON 4.3: BELOW

HYPO—HIPPO

Sub comes from Latin and gives meaning to words like submerge. *Under* comes from Old English and defines something that does not measure up or is below the standard in some way. *Hyp* and *hypo* come from Greek and are typically used with medical words.

Beginning	Root Word	Ending	New Word	Definition
sub	standard	substandard	below standards or of poor quality
sub	marine	submarine	under water; an underwater vessel
sub	urb	suburb	outlying part of a city
under	age	underage	of lower age, a minor
under	line	underline	to draw a line beneath
under	ground	underground	below the surface of ground; hidden or secret
hypo	dermic	hypodermic	under the skin; a needle used to give a shot
hypo	thesis	hypothesis	the assumed or unproven basis for an argument

FILL IN THE BLANK

Instructions: Use the words for Lesson 4.3 to complete the sentences below.

1. Scientists must state their _____ before conducting an

   experiment.

2. Towns that are outside of the city are called _____ .

3. My dad told me to bury my time capsule _____ .

4. My mom uses a _____ to give my grandmother an insulin

   injection for her diabetes each day.

THINKING ABOUT VOCABULARY

Looking at the root words for below, is it any surprise that the train system that takes passengers *under* a city like New York City or London is called the *sub*way? *Sub* and *under* are two root words used in much of our culture and everyday language. Fill in the boxes below to suggest additional common words that use *sub* or *under* as their roots.

sub
_____
_____
_____

under
_____
_____
_____

LESSON 4.4: INSIDE AND OUTSIDE

INSIDE

The prefixes for inside are *in*, *intro*, and *en/em* (Greek). These roots show that something is interior, turning inwards, detailing, or a call from within.

Beginning	Root Word	Ending	New Word	Definition
in	cline	incline	slope, slant; to lean toward
in	sect	insect	small animal whose body looks as if it is cut ("sect") into three parts
intro	duce	introduce	to "lead inwards"; to present or put into use
en	courage	encourage	literally, to put courage into someone
en	thusiasm	enthusiasm	divine inspiration; excitement
em	broider	embroider	to decorate with needlework

OUTSIDE

Roots for outside are *e*, *ex*, *exo*, and *ec*. They are from Greek and Latin and show when a word refers to something going out, wiped out, removed, made hollow, or not normal.

Beginning	Root Word	Ending	New Word	Definition
e	ject	eject	to throw out
ex	it	exit	the way out (n.); to go out (v.)
ex	pel	expel	push out
ec	centric	eccentric	odd person (n.); odd, strange behavior (adj.)

MAKE A WORD

Instructions: Match the correct root word and ending together to make seven words. For example, the root word "non" and the ending "agon" together make the word "nonagon." The root words and endings will be used only once!

Root Word	Ending	New Word
in	courage	
e	broider	
en	ject	
intro	cline	
ex	duce	
em	centric	
ec	it	

OUTSIDE OR INSIDE?

Instructions: Using the words in this lesson and your dictionary, decide which words in the word bank go with each definition. Then, write the words referring to "inside" in the center of the circle. Place the words referring to "outside" on the outside of the circle. Use this graphic organizer to help you the next time you need to remember the difference between "inside" and "outside" words. Be careful! Some of the words may be new to you!

Word Bank: index, enthusiastic, insect, expel, eject, exhale, embassy, enclose

1. small animal whose body is cut into parts
2. safe house for citizens of one country located inside another country
3. push out
4. excited
5. to breathe out
6. to throw or force out
7. a listing of the topics contained within a book
8. to fence off

LESSON 4.5: BETWEEN, NEAR, AND FAR

BETWEEN

The combining form for between is *inter* and is shown in words such as interrupt.

Beginning	Root Word	Ending	New Word	Definition
	inter	nal	internal	having to do with the inside or within
	inter	state	interstate	a public highway that connects one state to others; between states

NEAR

Proxim comes from Latin and means near.

Beginning	Root Word	Ending	New Word	Definition
	proxim	al	proximal	situated close by
ap	proxim	ate	approximate	to come close to; nearly; about

FAR

The root words that mean far are *tele* (Greek), *extra* (Latin), and *ultra* (Latin).

Beginning	Root Word	Ending	New Word	Definition
	tele	scope	telescope	an instrument used to increase distance so one can see objects far away
	tele	photo	telephoto	a lens to make distant objects appear closer
	tele	vision	television	literally, viewing things from far away; a tool to receive sight and sound
	extra	galactic	extragalactic	outside of the galaxy
	ultra	violet	ultraviolet	color beyond violet on the light spectrum
	ultra	sonic	ultrasonic	frequency of sounds beyond human hearing capability

THINKING ABOUT VOCABULARY

Both the roots *inter* and *tele* are commonly used in our everyday language. Think about words you use that have these roots. Then, write three other words for each root in the boxes below.

inter

tele

FILL IN THE BLANK

Instructions: Use the words in the tables for Lesson 4.5 to complete the sentences below.

1. The online map gave us an _____ distance of how far we

   needed to drive to get to Disneyland.

2. My sister had permission to drive on the _____ once she

   received her license.

3. In drama class the teacher told me to use my _____ emotions.

4. Sunglasses can help protect your eyes from the sun's _____

   rays.

5. One day, spacecraft may be _____ and allow us to travel

   beyond the Milky Way, the professor explained.

LESSON 4.6: CENTER, HIGH/SHARP

CENTER

Centr comes from Latin *centrum* and Greek *kentron*, meaning a sharp point in the middle of a circle.

Beginning	Root Word	Ending	New Word	Definition
	centr	alize	centralize	to gather toward a center
con	centr	ic	concentric	circles having a common center
epi	center		epicenter	the surface above the center of an earthquake

HIGH/SHARP

Alti (from Latin *altum*) and *acro* (Greek) are forms for high locations.

Beginning	Root Word	Ending	New Word	Definition
	alti	meter	altimeter	instrument for measuring height
	alt	o	alto	lowest-pitched female or the highest-pitched male voice
	acro	polis	acropolis	high or upper part of city
	acro	nym	acronym	a word formed from the first letters of several other words

MATCHING

Instructions: Match the words to their definitions.

Words
1. altimeter
2. acropolis
3. centralize
4. acronym

Definitions
a. to gather toward a center
b. word formed from the first letters of other words
c. high part of a city
d. instrument for measuring height

PICK THE WORD

Instructions: Circle the best word or phrase that completes each sentence.

1. The Philadelphia Boys Choir featured a solo alto performance by Seth, whose *(high, low, loud)* voice echoed in the choir hall.

2. The surface above the *(crust, atmosphere, center)* of the Earth is called the epicenter.

3. The *(acropolis, metropolis, acronym)* of the city was located at the top of a very steep and snowy hillside.

4. In geometry class we practiced drawing concentric circles, making sure they shared the same *(diameter, edge, center)*.

LESSON 4.7: BESIDE/ALONGSIDE AND AROUND

BESIDE/ALONGSIDE

Para comes from Greek and determines when a word's meaning is beside or alongside something else. This prefix also can signify that something is distinct.

Beginning	Root Word	Ending	New Word	Definition
	para	llel	parallel	two things running beside each other; lines that "go on forever" and remain the same distance apart
	para	site	parasite	a usually harmful animal or plant that lives on another (e.g., fleas)
	para	graph	paragraph	divides writing into sections

AROUND

The prefix forms for round are *peri* (Greek) and *circu/circum* (Latin). These forms can be found in words that describe the outside edge, as well as more interesting interpretations, such as something performed in rings (circus).

Beginning	Root Word	Ending	New Word	Definition
	peri	scope	periscope	instrument used to look above the surface of water while you are under water
	peri	meter	perimeter	distance around a figure or building
	circu	it	circuit	a complete electrical or other loop
	circu	s	circus	a traveling show often featuring acrobats, trained animals, clowns, and other acts that perform in tented rings

ANALOGIES

Instructions: Using the words and definitions in this lesson, choose the best word to finish each analogy.

1. one location : zoo : : traveling locations : _____

2. ⊥ : perpendicular : : ‖ : _____

3. _____ : essay : : line : drawing

WEB QUIZ

Instructions: Try your hand at creating words! Connect the correct root word listed in the inner circle to the word parts listed in the outer circles. You may have to use a root word more than once!

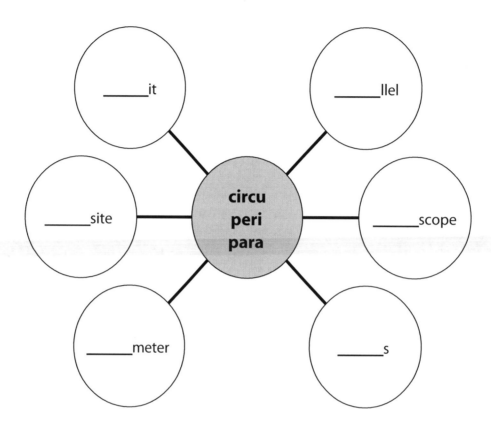

Rockin' Root Words Book 1 © Prufrock Press Inc. • Permission is granted to photocopy or reproduce this page for single classroom use only.

LESSON 4.B: TOWARD/TO AND AWAY

TOWARD/TO

Ad acts as a prefix when it is attached to a verb and means direction toward.

Beginning	Root Word	Ending	New Word	Definition
	ad	d	add	to join or unite something to something else to make it greater
	ad	verb	adverb	part of speech that adds information or modifies a verb
	ad	jective	adjective	part of speech that adds information or modifies a noun or pronoun
	ad	mire	admire	to show affection for; to look up to someone or something
	ad	here	adhere	to cling to

AWAY

The prefixes for away are *ab* and *apo* and may mean rejection, removal, and defense and response.

Beginning	Root Word	Ending	New Word	Definition
	ab	normal	abnormal	not normal
	ab	rasion	abrasion	a scraping or rubbing off
	apo	logy	apology	originally, a defense used in speeches; now, an admission of wrongs committed and a request for forgiveness
	apo	strophe	apostrophe	a punctuation mark used in contractions or to show ownership, as in "Sasha's book"

MATCHING

Instructions: Match the root words to their definitions.

Words

1. apo
2. ad
3. ab

Definitions

a. toward/to

b. away

SCRAMBLER

Instructions: Unscramble each word listed below. Use the clues to help you decipher the words.

drvaeb
(modifies a verb)

oibasanr
(scraping off)

haosroppet
(possessive
punctuation mark)

eaehdr
(stick to)

midear
(look up to)

yalgoop
(admitting you're
wrong)

oranbalm
(not typical)

Rockin' Root Words Book 1 © Prufrock Press Inc. • Permission is granted to photocopy or reproduce this page for single classroom use only.

LESSON 4.9: DOWN AND THROUGH/ACROSS

CAT-A-LOG

DOWN

Cata (Greek) means down, as in catastrophe, while *de* (Latin through French) means the bottom and down, as in descend.

Beginning	Root Word	Ending	New Word	Definition
cata	log	catalog	a list of things put down on paper
cata	pult	catapult	ancient machine used in throwing stones, logs, and other things at an enemy; to fly
de	press	depress	to put or push down
de	plane	deplane	to get off a plane

THROUGH/ACROSS

The prefixes for through and across are *tra* and *trans* (Latin) and *dia* (Greek and Latin). These prefixes offer clues about a word referring to something that moves through, changes, or crosses.

Beginning	Root Word	Ending	New Word	Definition
trans	late	translate	to change from one language into another
trans	atlantic	transatlantic	across the Atlantic Ocean
trans	form	transform	to change shape or form
tra	dition	tradition	something handed down, such as a belief
dia	meter	diameter	a line segment passing from one side to the other through the center of a circle or sphere
dia	gram	diagram	a figure marked with lines, such as a picture or visual aid

WEB QUIZ

Instructions: Try your hand at creating words! Connect the correct root word listed in the inner circle to the word parts listed in the outer circles. You may have to use a root word more than once!

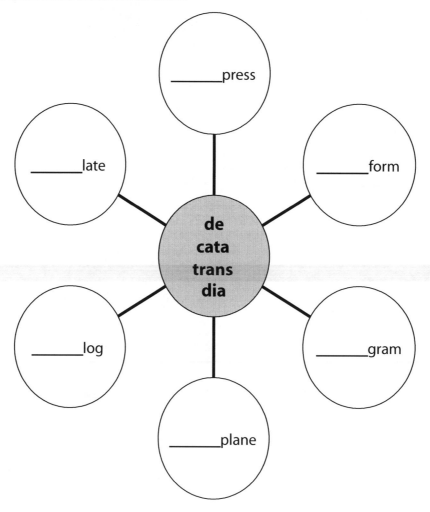

WHAT DOESN'T BELONG?

Instructions: Choose the word in each line that *does not* mean the same as the first word.

1. **diagram**   figure   visual aid   paragraph

2. **depress**   lift up   put down   push down

3. **transform**   change   stay the same   make different

4. **tradition**   artifact   custom   belief

5. **catapult**   to throw   to fly   to fall

LESSON 4.10: BACK/AGAIN

The prefixes for again are *re* (Latin through French) and *ana* (Greek). Knowing this root helps you know when a word refers to doing something again, holding, and happening again.

Beginning	Root Word	Ending	New Word	Definition
	re	act	react	to act in response
	re	late	relate	to give an account; to transfer information from one person to another
	re	cede	recede	to turn back, to lose ground
	re	flect	reflect	to turn back or throw back as light, heat, or sound waves; to consider carefully
	re	vise	revise	to look again or make changes
	re	verse	reverse	to turn backwards (v.); the back or opposite (adj.)
	ana	logy	analogy	a similarity of some aspects of otherwise different things
	ana	gram	anagram	a rearrangement of letters in a word to make a new word

GUESS THE MEANING

Instructions: For each word below, guess its meaning, writing your guess in the second column. Then, look up the word in a dictionary and write the real meaning in the third column.

word	I think it means . . .	It really means . . .
rewrite		
recharge		
rebound		
rerun		
reconsider		
reset		
refill		

WEB QUIZ

Instructions: Try your hand at creating words! Connect the correct root word listed in the inner circle to the word parts listed in the outer circles. You may have to use a root word more than once!

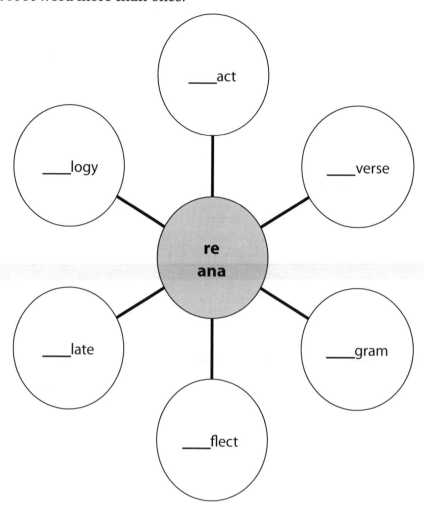

CHAPTER 4 REVIEW

ROOT WORDS MAD LIB

Instructions: This isn't your typical mad lib! Use the words in this chapter and the clues below to fill in the list of required words. Then, read the story on the next page replacing the blanks with your words to complete this silly tale of adventure on your summer vacation!

Clues for Word Bank

1. your name _____

2. your friend's name _____

3. exceedingly full _____

4. place, spot _____

5. place to go out _____

6. outlying part of a city

   _____

7. highway between states

   _____

8. below ground _____

9. not normal _____

10. to go back, backwards _____

11. slope, slant _____

12. change shape or form

   _____

13. your state's name _____

14. pick a color _____

15. engine of a railroad train

   _____

16. upper part of a city _____

17. pick an adjective _____

18. pick a type of clothing _____

19. traveling show performed in rings

   _____

20. circles connected by a center

   _____

21. pick a color _____

22. a contraption that makes things fly

   _____

23. your teacher's name _____

24. your friend's name _____

What I Did On My Summer Vacation

By: _____
(1)

My summer vacation started off quite normal, when my friend _____
(2)

invited me to go on a road trip. "Where are we going?" I asked excitedly as I got in the

car, with my _____ing bags packed and ready to go. "It's a secret
(3)

_____," my friend answered. "They won't tell us anything!" As we neared
(4)

the _____ of our _____, I began to get goosebumps. Something
(5)   (6)

told me this weekend was about to be great! We spent a few hours driving along the

_____ before entering a long, _____ tunnel. The tunnel was so
(7)   (8)

dark, it seemed frighteningly _____. My friend's mother, who was driving,
(9)

stepped on the brakes and tried to put the car in _____, but the cars
(10)

behind her starting honking loudly. We had to go on, but we were all creeped out! After

a steep _____, we made our way out of the tunnel. The world had completely
(11)

_____ed! We weren't in _____ anymore! And the huge
(12)   (13)

_____ _____ barreling toward us was proof of that! The car
(14)   (15)

swerved as we barely missed slamming into the train. Instead, we careened right up a

huge hill and into what looked like the world's _____—a huge city with
(16)

_____ buildings and people in matching _____ everywhere. Right
(17)   (18)

in the middle was a giant tent. "Well," my friend's mom said, "I was going to take you all

to the _____anyway, so we might as well make the most of it." I gulped
(19)

nervously as we entered the tent doors. Two _____ rings connected in
(20)

the center to showcase a huge _____ _____! With a bang, a
(21)   (22)

person came flying out! It was my teacher, _____! I rubbed my eyes in
(23)

surprise—Was this real? And, then, I heard someone yelling my name. _____
(24)

was suddenly in my bedroom, waking me up to go on our summer vacation.

CHAPTER 5

Shapes, Colors, Qualities

This chapter covers the many borrowed roots we use to describe shapes, and different kinds of shapes from straight, or crooked, to flat, or twisted. This chapter also covers both colors and qualities— or other ways in which we describe the objects around us.

Color makes up much of what we see in the world. With the exception of some rare people who cannot see certain colors, color makes us happy, dazzles our eyes, makes our mouths water, and helps us identify everyday objects. Do you think you'd like to eat a blue spotted banana, or perhaps green eggs? Though they might be delicious, your pushing away food like that would be understandable. Color is the way many animals, humans included, are able to decide what is safe to eat, and that's no small advantage!

When we are children, some of the first words we learn are words to describe what we want or what we see. Concepts like good and bad, same and different, hard and soft, heavy and light are ones that we sense in our infancy, even before we know the words for them.

LESSON 5.1: SHAPES

WELL, MY MOM
SAYS YOU'RE A FIGMENT
OF MY IMAGINATION!

The Latin roots for shape are *fig*, *fac(e)*, and *form*. The roots form words with meanings that indicate likeness, represent figures, or show the outside part or face of an object.

Beginning	Root Word	Ending	New Word	Definition
	fig	ure	figure	likeness, shape, form, or number
	fig	urine	figurine	a small sculpture or molded figure
dis	**fig**	ure	disfigure	to spoil the appearance or shape of
pre	**fac(e)**		preface	introduction to a book (n.), or to begin (v.)
	fac(e)	ial	facial	pertaining to the face (adj.); a treatment enhancing the skin of the face (n.)
con	**form**		conform	to adapt and agree
de	**form**		deform	to disfigure; to put out of shape
uni	**form**		uniform	one or the same form, alike, homogeneous (adj.); distinctive outfit worn by members of a group (n.)

WEB QUIZ

Instructions: Try your hand at creating words! Connect the correct root word listed in the inner circle to the word parts listed in the outer circles. You may have to use a root word more than once!

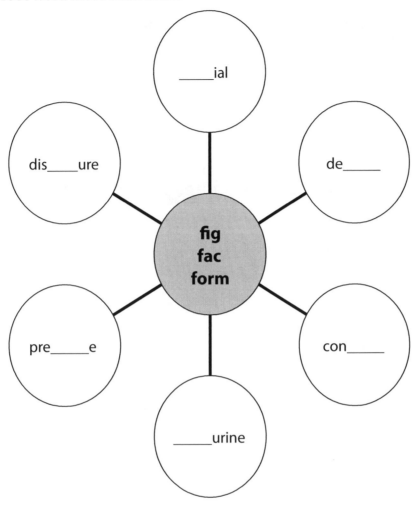

FILL IN THE BLANK

Instructions: Use the words for Lesson 5.1 to complete the sentences below.

1. John, my little brother, has a GI Joe action _____ in his room.

2. Girls sometimes go to salons to get a _____ and massage to relax.

3. The _____ contained a mysterious letter from one of the main

    characters, which set the scene for the rest of the novel.

4. I had to _____ to her wishes; the arguing and disagreement was

    giving me a headache.

5. The accident gave Maya a long, jagged scar that _____ her arm.

6. Everyone at the party wore black and white making it look as though we were in

    _____ .

LESSON 5.2: STRAIGHT AND LEVEL/FLAT

STRAIGHT

Ortho (Latin through French) is used in medical words for the science of straightening.

Beginning	Root Word	Ending	New Word	Definition
	ortho	pedics	orthopedics	branch of medicine treating diseases and injuries of the bones and joints
	ortho	dontist	orthodontist	dentist that fixes uneven teeth

LEVEL/FLAT

Plan, *plain* (Latin), *platy*, and *plat* are root forms for smooth, straight, level, or flat.

Beginning	Root Word	Ending	New Word	Definition
	plan	e	plane	a flat, level, and even surface
	plain		plain	large level land area (n.); simple, ordinary, common, frank, obvious, clear (adj.)
	plat	e	plate	a dish or a flat piece of metal; full-page illustration in a book

MATCHING

Instructions: Match the root words to their definitions.

Words
1. plain
2. plat
3. ortho
4. plan

Definitions
a. level/flat
b. straight

PICK THE WORD

Instructions: Circle the best word or phrase that completes each sentence.

1. We always use glass (*plates, planes, plastic*) when we eat.

2. When my teammate sprained his ankle, our coach advised him to see an (*orthodontist, orthopedic, orthodox*) surgeon.

3. The chips didn't have any salt, making them taste rather (*plane, plan, plain*).

4. My mother took me to the (*orthodontist, orthodoctor, orthopedics*) to see about getting my teeth straightened.

5. My niece was so scared to get on the (*airplain, airport, airplane*).

LESSON 5.3: ROUND, WHEEL-LIKE, AND EGG-SHAPED

ROUND

Round comes from Latin through French and appears in English in the obvious forms of roundup, rounded, and other similar words.

Beginning	Root Word	Ending	New Word	Definition
	round		round	circular or spherical
	round	about	roundabout	not straightforward, indirect, circuitous

WHEEL-LIKE

Rot comes from Latin to describe wheel-like shapes or objects. This root helps you decipher when a word's meaning refers to the circular shape of a wheel or the motion of a wheel.

Beginning	Root Word	Ending	New Word	Definition
	rot	unda	rotunda	round building, hall, or room usually with a dome above it
	rot	ation	rotation	revolving or rolling motion

EGG-SHAPED

Ov derives from Latin and can be found in words referring to eggs or egg shapes.

Beginning	Root Word	Ending	New Word	Definition
	ov	oid	ovoid	egg-shaped
	ov	al	oval	egg-shaped

WEB QUIZ

Instructions: Try your hand at creating words! Connect the correct root word listed in the inner circle to the word parts listed in the outer circles. You may have to use a root word more than once!

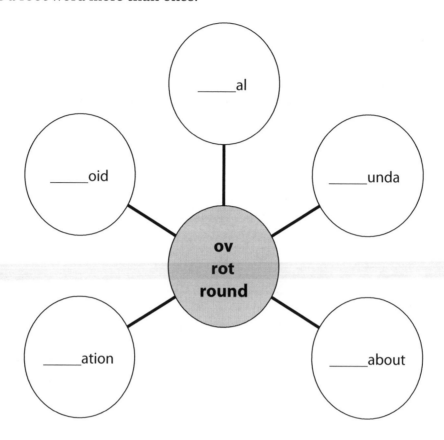

PICTURING VOCABULARY

Instructions: Use the prompts below to draw or locate pictures that represent this lesson's vocabulary words. Draw your illustrations on another piece of paper.

1. Draw an object from your everyday life that is round.

2. Many things rotate, including the Earth. Draw or find a picture of something that rotates that is not the Earth.

3. A rotunda is a round-shaped room, building, or hall. Most state capitols have rotundas. Go online and find pictures of your state capitol (don't forget to get permission and help from your teacher or a family member). Print a picture and paste or staple it to the back of this sheet.

LESSON 5.4: WHITE/SILVER AND GOLD

WHITE/SILVER

The roots for silver are *alb* (Latin) and *argent* (Latin through French).

Beginning	Root Word	Ending	New Word	Definition
	alb	um	album	Roman writing tablet where public announcements were made; now, it is a notebook for pictures or drawings
	alb	atross	albatross	large, white sea-bird
	argent	ina	Argentina	the "Silver Republic," named for the silver jewelry worn by the natives at the time of the Europeans' arrival

GOLD

The combining form for gold or gold-colored is *chrys*.

Beginning	Root Word	Ending	New Word	Definition
	chrys	alis	chrysalis	insect pupa enclosed in a shell
	chrys	anthemum	chrysanthemum	a type of flower that often is golden

FILL IN THE BLANK

Instructions: Use the words for Lesson 5.4 to complete the sentences below.

1. My admirer bought me a golden flower called a _____.

2. To track my family genealogy, I used a picture _____of my family dating back to the 1800s.

3. We learned in history class that the "Silver Republic" is the nickname for the South American country of _____.

MAKE A WORD

Instructions: Match the correct root word and ending together to make four words. For example, the root word "non" and the ending "agon" together make the new word "nonagon." The root words and endings can be used more than once.

Root Word	Ending	New Word
alb	alis	
chrys	ina	
argent	atross	
	anthemum	

LESSON 5.5: RED, PINK, BLUE, AND GREEN

RED

Rub and *rubr* come from Latin to mean red.

Beginning	Root Word	Ending	New Word	Definition
	rub	y	ruby	red gemstone
	rub	ella	rubella	small, usually mild red rash

PINK

Rhod comes from Greek to mean pink or rose.

Beginning	Root Word	Ending	New Word	Definition
	rhod	odendron	rhododendron	literally, "rose tree" in Greek; the plant does not have roses, but flowers in shades of pink, red, and other colors

GREEN

Chlor comes from Greek to mean green.

Beginning	Root Word	Ending	New Word	Definition
	chlor	ophyll	chlorophyll	green pigment found in plant cells

BLUE

Cyan comes from Greek to mean blue.

Beginning	Root Word	Ending	New Word	Definition
	cyan	ide	cyanide	poisonous chemical salt used in extracting gold from its ore

MATCHING

Instructions: Match the root words to their definitions.

Words	Definitions
1. cyan	a. red
2. rhod	b. green
3. rub	c. pink
4. chlor	d. blue

SCRAMBLER

Instructions: Unscramble each word listed below. Use the clues to help you decipher the words.

decainy
(poisonous chemical)

ryub
(gem)

labelur
(mild rash)

nehoodndrdro
(tree)

rlolhophycl
(pigment)

LESSON 5.6: GOOD/WELL AND BAD/WRONG/NOT

GOOD/WELL

The combining forms are *bene* and *bon* (Latin) and *eu* (Greek). These roots find homes in words that describe the relative goodness of objects, people, and situations.

Beginning	Root Word	Ending	New Word	Definition
	bene	fit	benefit	something advantageous or good
	bene	ficial	beneficial	that which benefits something or someone
	bon	us	bonus	a prize or unexpected reward
	eu	logy	eulogy	speech given at a funeral; speaking well of the dead

BAD/WRONG/NOT

The combining forms are *mis*, *mal(e)*, *dis*, *dys*, and *dif* (Latin). These roots form the English words for bad, wrong, not, and for something that should not have happened.

Beginning	Root Word	Ending	New Word	Definition
	mis	fortune	misfortune	bad luck
	mal	formed	malformed	badly-formed
	dis	aster	disaster	a horrible occurrence or tragedy
	dis	turb	disturb	to cause disorder; upset
	dys	lexia	dyslexia	difficulty in reading certain words or letters
	dif	fer	differ	to be unlike; to disagree

ANALOGIES

Instructions: Using the words and definitions in this lesson, choose the best word to finish each analogy.

1. _____ : funeral : : acceptance speech : awards show

2. dysgraphia : difficulty with writing : : _____ : difficulty with reading

3. agree : _____ : : good : evil

4. earthquake : _____ : : cumulus : cloud

5. tournament champion : trophy : : hard worker : _____

THINKING ABOUT VOCABULARY

Instructions: When we use the word *disaster*, we are actually drawing on the ancient belief that says that stars (*aster*) determine a person's future. Answer the following questions about this lesson's vocabulary, including the word disaster.

1. If someone has the opposite of good luck, what would you call it?

   _____

2. There are many things in life that we take for granted, including being young. What are three benefits of being a child?

   _____

   _____

   _____

3. Natural disasters affect people on a regular basis around the world, regardless of where they live and what they have. Such disasters can change everything in an instant. On a separate piece of paper, write a letter to the victim of a natural disaster. Be sure to give them encouragement and share information about yourself.

LESSON 5.7: SAME AND DIFFERENT

SAME/ALMOST THE SAME

The Greek root for sameness is *homo*; the Latin root is *simul*. These roots give you a clue about when a word's meaning pertains to a quality of sameness or of near sameness.

Beginning	Root Word	Ending	New Word	Definition
	homo	phone	homophone	two or more words having the same pronunciation but different meanings (e.g., sight and site)
	homo	nym	homonym	words that sound alike and are spelled alike but have different meanings (e.g., left and left)
	simil	ar	similar	state of being like another thing
	simil	e	simile	a literary term featuring a stated comparison
fac	simil	e	facsimile	a copy, a likeness (a short form is "fax")
	simul	ator	simulator	a testing device to create conditions in a lab similar to real conditions

DIFFERENT/OTHER

The roots used to portray different qualities are *hetero* (Greek) and *ali/alle* (Latin). These prefixes in English express differences or contrasts between people, objects, and concepts.

Beginning	Root Word	Ending	New Word	Definition
	hetero	geneous	heterogeneous	of different kinds
	ali	bi	alibi	the legal defense that someone else knows the accused was away from the scene of a crime when it took place; thus, he or she could not possibly have committed the crime
	ali	en	alien	stranger or foreigner (n.); strange (adj.)
	alle	rgy	allergy	a sensitivity to a specific substance that causes a reaction, like a rash

WEB QUIZ

Instructions: Try your hand at creating words! Connect the correct root word listed in the inner circle to the word parts listed in the outer circles. You may have to use a root word more than once!

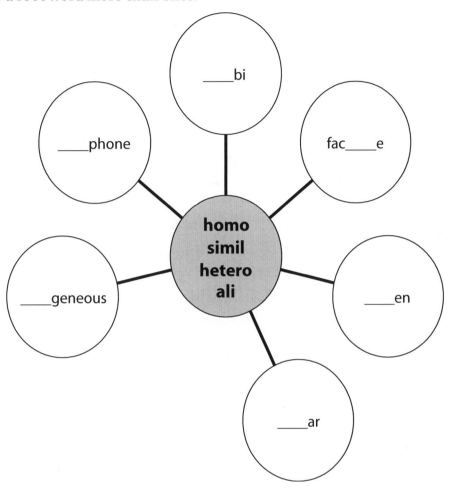

TRUE OR FALSE

Instructions: Read the statements below and, using your vocabulary from this lesson, decide if they are true or false.

1. If two animals are heterogeneous, they are of the same species.   **T**   **F**
2. "The rain sounded like tap dancers on my tin roof" is an example of a   **T**   **F**
   simile.
3. The words "their" and "there" show an example of a homophone.   **T**   **F**
4. If someone moves to a foreign country he is considered an "alien."   **T**   **F**
5. A simulator is used to help scientists create conditions similar to lab   **T**   **F**
   conditions.
6. Darek was present at the scene of the crime, therefore the judge   **T**   **F**
   considered him to have an alibi for the theft.

CHAPTER 5 WRAP-UP

CROSSWORD PUZZLE

Instructions: Use the definitions in the clues on the following page to complete the crossword puzzle.

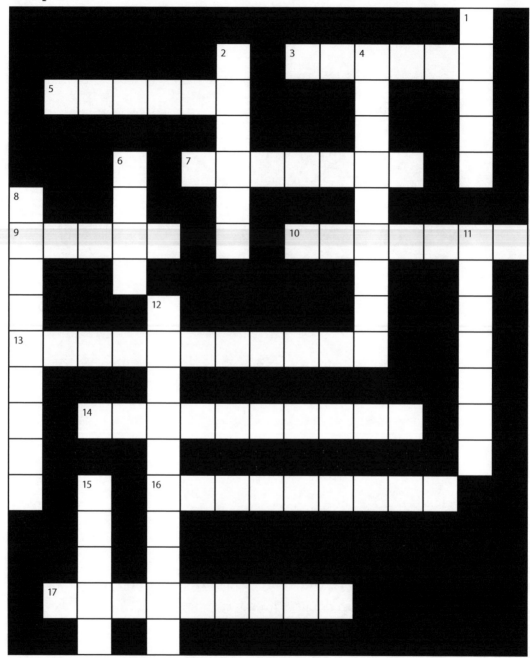

ACROSS

3. pertaining to the face
5. likeness, shape, form
7. words that sound alike and are spelled alike but mean different things (e.g., rose and rose)
9. legal defense that states you could not have committed a crime
10. poisonous substance
13. treatment for joints and bones
14. that which benefits someone
16. large white sea bird
17. testing device that aims to create real conditions

DOWN

1. large, flat land area
2. to disfigure
4. insect pupa enclosed in a shell
6. red gemstone
8. badly formed
11. to cause disorder
12. a roadway that's not straight
15. egg-shaped

CHAPTER 6

Bodily Structures and Senses

For its time, Greek medicine was the most advanced in the world. Although many of their medical theories have been proven false, the Greeks' attention to detail and careful observations set the standard for medical practice for hundreds of years. The Romans learned from the Greeks and, as a result, much of the medical terminology they used has become part of our medical and body vocabulary.

The five senses are among the few *native* English words that we use every day. Smell comes from the Old English *smyllan*; taste comes from the Middle English *tasten*; hear comes from the Old English *hieren*; touch comes from the Middle English *touchen*; and see comes from the Old English *seon*. Words for objects or concepts that are physically closest to us, or that have to do directly with our personal being, tend to stay our own in origin. If English is so willing to adopt or borrow foreign words, why do certain categories of words remain our own after hundreds of years of mixing with foreign languages?

LESSON 6.1: ORGANS AND HEART

ORGANS

Organ derives from Greek and Latin and, as a root, it has come to mean not only organ, but also system.

Beginning	Root Word	Ending	New Word	Definition
	organ		organ	specialized tissue in the body that has a specific function; a musical instrument
	organ	ization	organization	an orderly system or structure; an organized group or business
	organ	ic	organic	pertaining to living organisms; basic, natural foods

HEART

The roots *card* (Greek), *cord* (Latin), and *cour* (French) all mean heart. These roots pertain to not only the actual organ of the heart, but also emotions of the heart.

Beginning	Root Word	Ending	New Word	Definition
	card	iac	cardiac	pertaining to the heart
	cord	ial	cordial	hearty, warm, and friendly (adj.); food or drink that stimulates the heart (n.)
dis	cord		discord	disagreement; lack of harmony
con	cord		concord	agreement
	cour	age	courage	bravery, fearlessness, valor

SYNONYM SEARCH

Instructions: Sort through the words in the word bank to find synonyms for the vocabulary words listed below. Write the synonyms on the lines next to the words they correspond with. Be careful—some of the words in the word bank will not be used!

> **Word Bank:** natural, disagreement, cold, fearless, specialized tissue, agreement, group, hearty

1. organization _____

2. discord _____

3. organ _____

4. organic _____

5. courageous _____

WORD MATH

Instructions: Read the instructions in the box in order to create a new word by changing the word before it. Use the clues at the bottom of the box to help you create the new words.

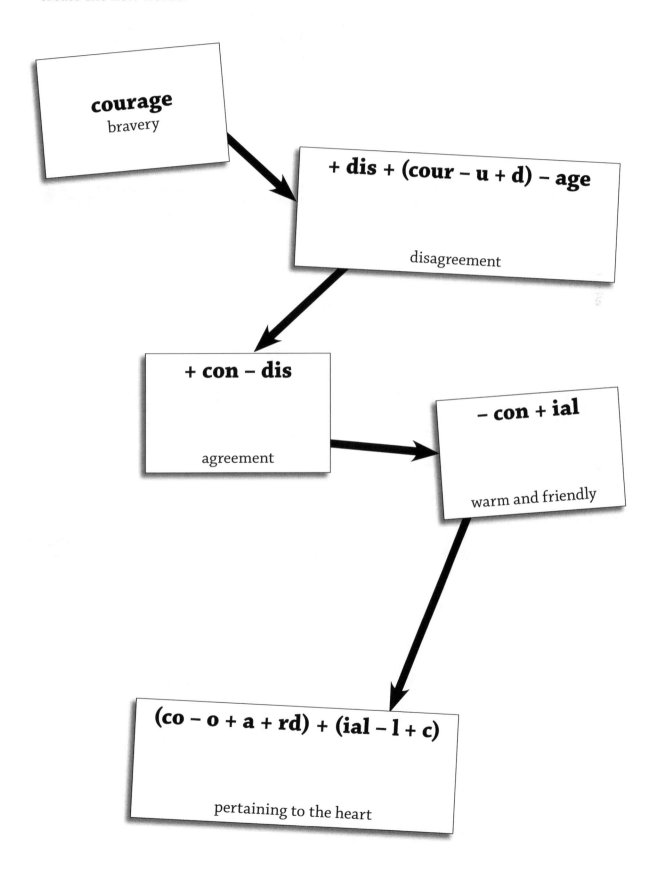

LESSON 6.2: HEAD, EYES, MOUTH, AND TEETH

HEAD

Cap comes from Latin to mean head or top of the body.

Beginning	Root Word	Ending	New Word	Definition
	cap		cap	close-fitting head covering; a cover or top
	cap	e	cape	hooded sleeveless top; piece of land going into the sea, headland

EYES

The root words for eye are *ocul/oc* and *opt*.

Beginning	Root Word	Ending	New Word	Definition
bin	ocul	ars	binoculars	a device for looking at distant objects with both eyes
mon	oc	le	monocle	eyeglass for one eye only
	opt	ician	optician	technician who checks eyesight for glasses
	opt	ical	optical	pertaining to vision

MOUTH

The Latin root for mouth is *or*, as in orthodontist.

Beginning	Root Word	Ending	New Word	Definition
	or	al	oral	verbally, by way of the mouth

TEETH

The Latin root for teeth is *dent*. This root appears in a wide variety of dental terms and is used to describe anything with pointed "teeth."

Beginning	Root Word	Ending	New Word	Definition
	dent	ist	dentist	tooth care specialist
	dent	ure	denture	artificial set of teeth

MATCHING

Instructions: Match the root words to their meanings.

Words	Definitions
1. or	a. teeth
2. opt	b. head
3. dent	c. eyes
4. cap	d. mouth
5. ocul	
6. oc	

FILL IN THE BLANK

Instructions: Use the words for Lesson 6.2 to complete the sentences below.

1. Because of my grandfather's old age, he lost some of his teeth and now has to wear a set of _____.

2. The _____ told me that I had near-sighted vision and needed to wear glasses.

3. Little Red Riding Hood wore a _____ and hood.

4. The doctor explained that I would need _____ surgery to fix my jaw.

Lesson 6.3: Hands and Fingers/Toes

HANDS

The root words for hands are *man(u)* (Latin), *chiro* (Greek), *dexter*, and *cap* (Latin).

Beginning	Root Word	Ending	New Word	Definition
	manu	al	manual	a handbook for directions (n.); made, done, or worked by hand (adj.)
	man	icure	manicure	care for the fingernails and hands
	man	age	manage	to conduct, oversee, control, get through
	man	ipulate	manipulate	to handle with skill, but sometimes implying unfair advantage
	chiro	practor	chiropractor	person who treats patients by manipulation of bone joints, especially the spine
	cap	ture	capture	to take by force (v.); the taking by force, seizure (n.)

FINGERS/TOES

Digit derives from Latin for fingers or toes. These roots appear in English words to represent appendages or what they can do.

Beginning	Root Word	Ending	New Word	Definition
	digit		digit	finger; any number from 0 to 9
	digit	al	digital	of the finger; relating to the electronic transmission of data, sounds, and images

PICK THE WORD

Instructions: Circle the best word or phrase that completes each sentence.

1. The photographer wanted to (*capture, capsize, captain*) the best

   photographs at the wedding reception.

2. My dad was such a good (*manipulator, manager, manual*) of his department

   at work that his employees nominated him for an award.

3. I had such severe back pain that I had to see a (*chiropractor, optician,*

   manicurist).

4. My friends and I like to get (*manuals, digits, manicures*) at the salon each

   month.

5. The camera only took (*manual, digital, capture*) pictures, so I had to load

   them on my computer and print them out at home.

WEB QUIZ

Instructions: Try your hand at creating words! Connect the correct root word listed in the inner circle to the word parts listed in the outer circles. You may have to use a root word more than once!

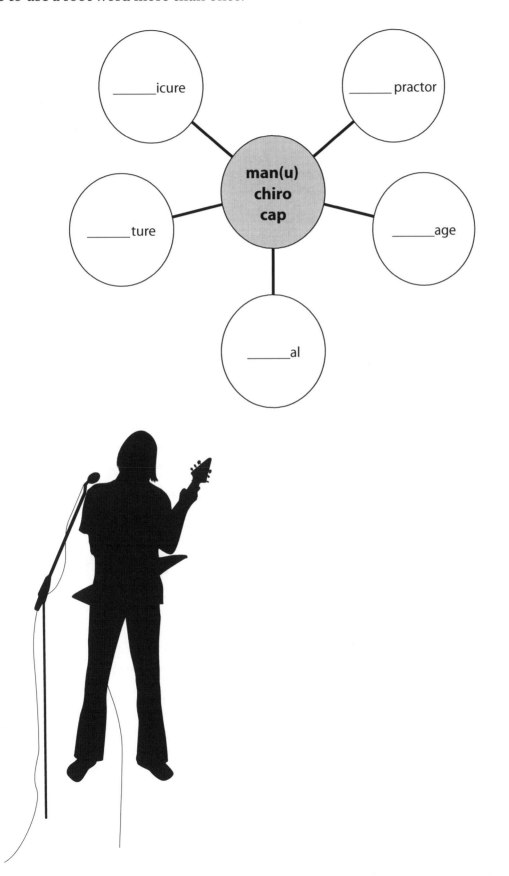

_____icure

_____practor

_____ture

man(u)
chiro
cap

_____age

_____al

LESSON 6.4: FEET

Root words for feet are *ped* (Latin through French), *pod* (Greek), and *pus* (Greek). These roots appear in English to describe walking or any other motion of the feet and feet alone.

Beginning	Root Word	Ending	New Word	Definition
mo	**ped**		moped	scooter (short for "motorized pedal")
	ped	icure	pedicure	care and treatment of feet
	ped	estrian	pedestrian	one who walks
bi	**ped**		biped	two-footed creature
ex	**ped**	ition	expedition	a journey or voyage
	pod	iatrist	podiatrist	doctor who cares for feet
	pod	ium	podium	a raised platform or low wall that serves as a pedestal or foundation
octo	**pus**		octopus	eight-footed marine animal

WORD SPLITS

Instructions: The makers of a new dictionary want to break up some words into their word parts for their new edition, but need your help! Can you divide the following words into their word parts? Think carefully—a few words may be new to you!

1. moped: _____ + _____

2. podium: _____ + _____

3. platypus: _____ + _____

4. octopus: _____ + _____

5. expedition: _____ + _____ + _____

6. antipodes: _____ + _____ + _____

WORD MATH

Instructions: Read the instructions in the box in order to create a new word by changing the word before it. Use the clues at the bottom of the box to help you create the new words.

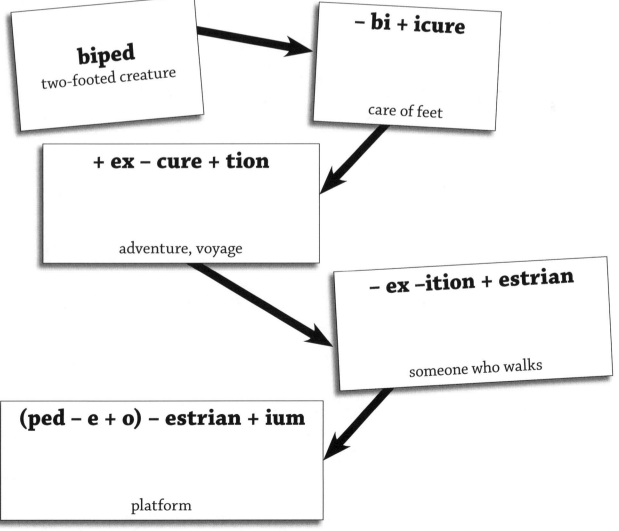

biped
two-footed creature

– bi + icure

care of feet

+ ex – cure + tion

adventure, voyage

– ex –ition + estrian

someone who walks

(ped – e + o) – estrian + ium

platform

LESSON 6.5: LIFE AND DEATH

LIFE

The roots for life are *viv* (Latin), *vit* (Latin), *zo* (Greek), and *bio* (Greek and Latin). These roots take on the additional meanings of vitality and of being necessary for life.

Beginning	Root Word	Ending	New Word	Definition
re	**viv**	e	revive	bring back to life again
sur	**viv**	e	survive	to endure hardship; to live another day
	vit	al	vital	belonging to life or necessary for life
	vit	amin	vitamin	a micronutrient essential for life
	zo	ology	zoology	science and study of animals
	bio	logy	biology	study of living organisms
	bio	graphy	graphy	history of someone's life

DEATH

Mort (Latin) is a root meaning the end or death.

Beginning	Root Word	Ending	New Word	Definition
	mort	al	mortal	a human being; something causing death like a wound
im	**mort**	al	immortal	living forever; deathless

FILL IN THE BLANK

Instructions: Use the words for Lesson 6.5 to complete the sentences below.

1. One of my favorite TV shows explores how people might

   _____ in the wilderness.

2. _____ is the study of all life forms.

3. Animals fascinate me so much that I have decided to study

   _____ when I go to college.

4. Unlike the Greek gods of mythology, who could live forever, human beings

   are _____.

WEB QUIZ

Instructions: Try your hand at creating words! Connect the correct root word listed in the inner circle to the word parts listed in the outer circles. You may have to use a root word more than once!

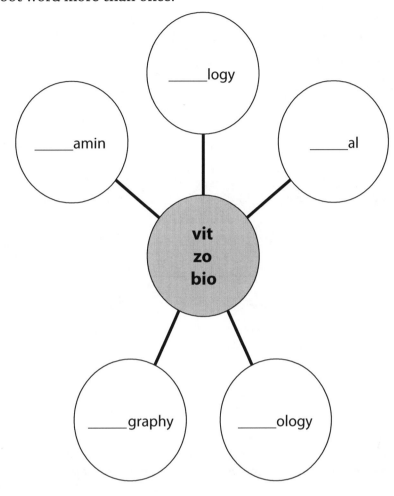

LESSON 6.6: BODY/FLESH

THE SARCASTIC SARCOPHAGUS

The root words for body and blood are *carn* (Latin), *corp* (Latin through French), and *sarc* (Latin through French). These roots find their home in the English words for flesh and many of the words with these roots represent death or decay.

Beginning	Root Word	Ending	New Word	Definition
	carn	ation	carnation	flower once considered flesh-colored
	carn	ivore	carnivore	flesh-eating animal
rein	**carn**	ation	reincarnation	rebirth of the soul in another body, as in Hindu belief
	corp	oration	corporation	a governing body or chartered business firm
	corp	se	corpse	dead body
	sarc	ophagus	sarcophagus	limestone coffin or tomb
	sarc	astic	sarcastic	having a piercing, caustic nature of mockery

MATCHING

Instructions: Match the root words to their meanings.

Words
1. corporation
2. sarcophagus
3. reincarnation
4. corpse

Definitions
a. rebirth of the soul in another body
b. dead body
c. coffin or tomb
d. business firm

CHANGE IT UP

Instructions: Replace the underlined word or words in each sentence with one of the vocabulary words in the word bank.

Word Bank: carnivores, sarcasm, corporation, carnations, sarcophagus

1. The state art museum had a rare <u>coffin</u> that was built for a member of the Egyptian royal family.
2. The <u>business</u> my dad works for has more than 600 employees.
3. For Valentine's Day, I helped out in the florist's workroom, sorting and cutting the stems of pink, red, and white <u>flowers</u>.
4. We saw many <u>meat-eaters</u> on our African safari this summer, including two beautiful lion cubs.
5. Her words stung with <u>mockery</u>, telling me she wasn't taking our conversation very seriously.

LESSON 6.7: SEEING AND LOOKING

Vi and *vis* come from Latin. *Scop* derives from Latin and Greek. These roots create words that mean sight, examining closely, and the obvious.

Beginning	Root Word	Ending	New Word	Definition
	vid	eo	video	filmed or taped performance or presentation
e	**vid**	ence	evidence	proof, grounds for belief; to bring proof to
pro	**vid**	e	provide	to supply, prepare for, or make a condition
	vis	ual	visual	connected to the sense of sight
in	**vis**	ible	invisible	pertaining to what cannot be seen
micro	**scop**	e	microscope	instrument for magnifying small objects for examination
tele	**scop**	e	telescope	instrument for viewing faraway objects
peri	**scop**	e	periscope	a device used in submarines to look above the surface of the water while under water

WEB QUIZ

Instructions: Try your hand at creating words! Connect the correct root word listed in the inner circle to the word parts listed in the outer circles. You may have to use a root word more than once!

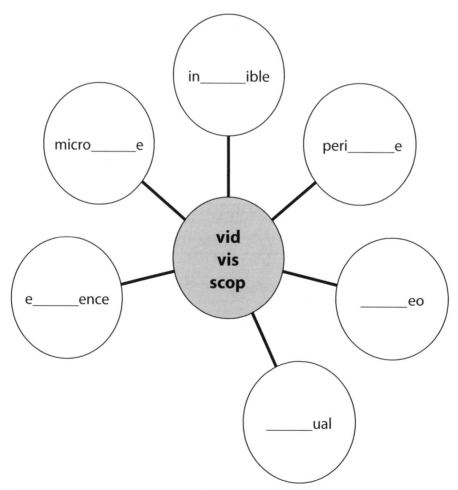

ALL MIXED UP

Instructions: Help! The following word parts were all mixed up in the dictionary. Connect the word parts by drawing lines between the boxes. Then, write the correct words in the lines next to their definitions. Be careful! Some of the connections can be tricky: You only want to find words that match the definitions below.

1. _____: used to view faraway objects

2. _____: proof

3. _____: cannot be seen

4. _____: can magnify small objects

5. _____: supply

6. _____: can be seen

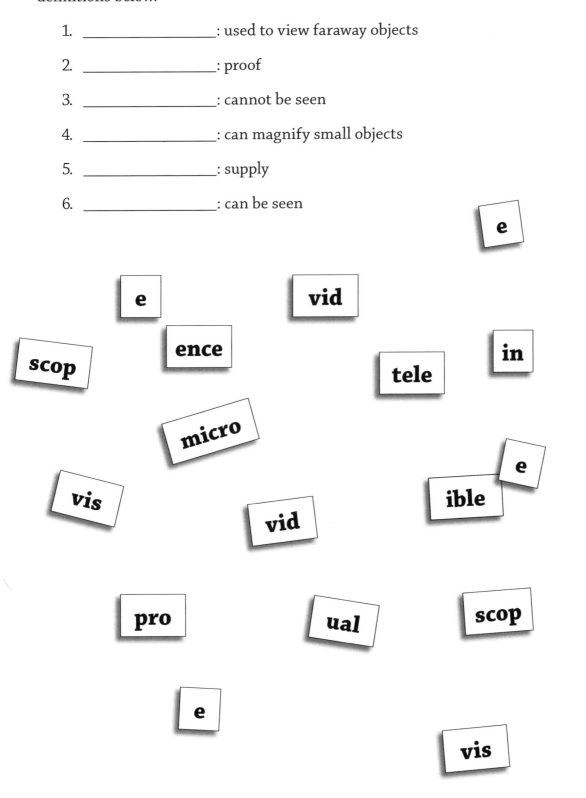

LESSON 6.8: HEARING AND SOUND

The roots for hearing and sound are *ton* (Latin), *son*, *phon* (Greek), and *aud* (Latin). They form the foundation of many words that pertain to hearing, sound, and music.

Beginning	Root Word	Ending	New Word	Definition
	ton	e	tone	a distinct musical or vocal sound; a style, trend, or atmosphere; the quality of color; a voice quality indicating mood or emotion
mono	**ton**	e	monotone	uninterrupted repetition of the same tone
	son	ogram	sonogram	record of an ultrasound test of a body part to check for illness
	son	ar	sonar	acronym for **SO**und **NA**vigation **R**ange
tele	**phon**	e	telephone	literally, sound from far away; a common sound communication device
micro	**phon**	e	microphone	an electrical device that amplifies sound
saxo	**phon**	e	saxophone	a certain musical reed instrument
	aud	itorium	auditorium	hall for an audience
	aud	ience	audience	group of people who gather to hear or see a speaker, play, or concert; a writer's readers

TELEPHONE CALL

Instructions: Your best friend had just called to share her day's events when your phone started breaking up! See if you can decipher her words below using the word parts provided or the clues in the paragraph in which the words appear.

You wouldn't believe what happened to me today. I was walking into the _____itorium after lunch for the talent show, and I was so shocked! The _____ was so big that it filled almost all of the seats. I immediately started getting nervous. You know how I am about stage fright! I took my place back stage and had to listen to the principal talk on and on into the _____. He has such a horrible _____tone voice that I nearly fell asleep! Then, it was finally my turn. I stepped up to the microphone, with my saxo_____ in hand, and started playing. To my surprise, a beautiful _____ poured out; it was such a distinct sound that everyone was enraptured. My butterflies seemed to go away! And, then, of course, my perfect moment was ruined—my _____ rang! Not only did everyone start laughing, but I got detention!

WEB QUIZ

Instructions: Try your hand at creating words! Connect the correct root word listed in the inner circle to the word endings listed in the outer circles. You may have to use a root word more than once!

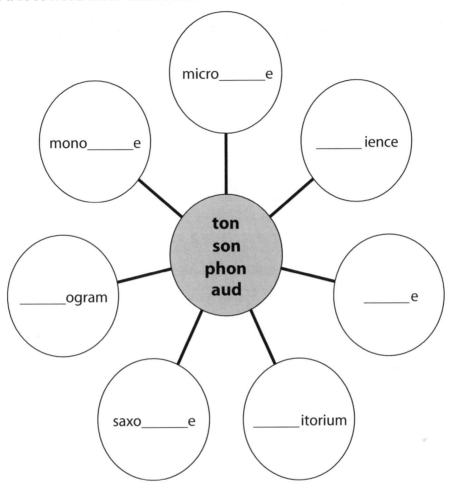

LESSON 6.9: TOUCH

The roots for touch are *tact* and *tang*. You also can use these roots to decipher words that mean the concept of briefly touching on a subject.

Beginning	Root Word	Ending	New Word	Definition
	tact		tact	poise, diplomacy, sensitivity
con	tact		contact	act of touching, meeting, or communicating; pertaining to physical touching; a person known to another
in	tact		intact	whole or untouched
	tang	ent	tangent	touching, but not crossing; off the main point; a trigonometry ratio
	tang	ible	tangible	that which can be touched; definite, clear

MATCHING

Instructions: Match the root words to their meanings.

Words
1. contact
2. tangible
3. tangent
4. tact

Definitions
a. definite
b. touch
c. sensitivity
d. off the point

FILL IN THE BLANK

Instructions: Use the words for Lesson 6.9 to complete the sentences below.

1. My science teacher told me to never make physical _____ with poisonous substances.

2. Something concrete and immediate versus vague and unreal is _____.

3. Jasmine tried to listen to the history lecture, but found it difficult as her teacher kept going off on a _____ about the latest political causes he was supporting.

4. "I think you handled the situation with _____ and respect," my mother said, praising me for my actions.

LESSON 6.10: FEELING

Two roots for feeling are *sens* and *sent*. Although not technically one of the five bodily senses, the roots for feeling are the source of various words relating to the bodily senses.

Beginning	Root Word	Ending	New Word	Definition
	sens	or	sensor	device which detects and measures physical changes in its environment
non	**sens**	e	nonsense	that which does not make sense; foolishness
	sens	itive	sensitive	having highly-tuned senses; able to detect minimal stimuli; emotionally sympathetic
	sent	ence	sentence	a group of words, which includes a subject and verb and expresses a complete thought
	sent	ry	sentry	a guard who keeps watch

PICK THE WORD

Instructions: Circle the best word or phrase that completes each sentence.

1. Edward Lear was a great writer of imaginative, unusual (*sensical, sensitive, nonsense*) poems that some considered quite foolish.

2. In English class we had to write a (*sentence, sentry, sensor*) for each of our new vocabulary words.

3. Emily is very (*sensible, sensitive, nonsensical*); she cries over everything.

GUESS THE MEANING

Instructions: For each word below, guess its meaning, writing your guess in the second column. Then, look up the word in a dictionary and write the real meaning in the third column.

word	I think it means . . .	It really means . . .
sensible		
sensory		
senseless		
sensational		
sentiment		

CHAPTER 6 WRAP-UP

A MATTER OF LIFE AND DEATH

Instructions: Using the vocabulary words listed below, write a short story about a mortal character who meets an immortal Greek god and must complete three tasks in order to save his or her family. Before starting your story, review the meanings of *mortal* and *immortal* in this chapter. Be as creative as possible, but make sure your vocabulary words are used correctly! You may use additional vocabulary words from this chapter if you'd like, and you may write or type your story on another piece of paper.

Word Bank: courage, cap, manage, capture, expedition, vital, sarcastic, evidence, tone, audience, intact, sentry

_____

_____

_____

_____

_____

_____

_____

_____

_____

_____

_____

_____

_____

_____

_____

_____

_____

CHAPTER 7

Self, Family, and Home Life

Our immediate family generally consists of mothers, fathers, brothers, and sisters. When people go to college, many young women join a sorority (sisterhood) and many young men join a fraternity (brotherhood). Marriage and children follow.

The rest of the chapter covers words associated with various home arts, including cooking. Roman home life centered on the father, or the *Pater Familias*. He would decide whether you would go to school, who and when you would marry, and all other important decisions that involved the entire family. That doesn't mean the *Mater Familias* or mother was without influence. In fact, Roman history is filled with accounts of powerful women who constituted the real "power behind the throne."

LESSON 7.1: SELF, MAN, AND WOMAN

SELF

The Greek roots for self are *auto* and *aut*. These roots signal that a word's meaning describes something to do with an individual's self or person.

Beginning	Root Word	Ending	New Word	Definition
	auto	mobile	automobile	a self-propelled passenger vehicle; motorcar
	auto	biography	autobiography	history of a person's life, written or told by the person; memoir
	auto	graph	autograph	one's own signature

MAN

Anthrop derives from Greek to mean man and forms the roots of words that refer to humankind.

Beginning	Root Word	Ending	New Word	Definition
	anthrop	ology	anthropology	the study of human beings and past civilizations

WOMAN

The Latin base for female is *femin*.

Beginning	Root Word	Ending	New Word	Definition
	femin	ine	feminine	being womanly; pertaining to women

MATCHING

Instructions: Match the root words to their meanings.

Words	Definitions
1. anthrop	a. womanly
2. auto	b. self
3. femin	c. human

CHANGE IT UP

Instructions: Replace the underlined word or words in each sentence with one of the vocabulary words in the word bank.

Word Bank: autobiography, autograph, feminine, anthropology

1. Another name for <u>signature</u> is a John Hancock, after one of the men who signed the *Declaration of Independence.*
2. My pink and white room has a very <u>womanly</u> atmosphere.
3. My older sister is traveling to Egypt to study the <u>human history</u> of its people.
4. The President recently penned his <u>memoir</u> of his life on the campaign trail.

LESSON 7.2: FATHER, MOTHER, AND CHILD

FATHER

Patr/pater comes from Latin through French and describes words meaning fathers or fatherhood. This root also carries the additional meaning of referring to the home.

Beginning	Root Word	Ending	New Word	Definition
	patr	on	patron	benefactor; person who gives money or support to others, particularly artists
	patr	iot	patriot	a person whose loyalties are to his or her home country

MOTHER

Matr/metro comes from Latin and refers to mothers and the state of motherhood.

Beginning	Root Word	Ending	New Word	Definition
	matr	on	matron	a mature woman who may manage a school, hospital, or other institution
	matr	imony	matrimony	marriage as a prelude to becoming a mother
	metro	polis	metropolis	literally, "mother city"; a large city

CHILD

Ped comes from Greek to mean child. English makes use of this root term to describe something that is related to children, deals with children, or is childish. This root also carries connotations of learning or study.

Beginning	Root Word	Ending	New Word	Definition
encyclo	**ped**	ia	encyclopedia	a book that covers all branches of knowledge
	ped	igree	pedigree	genealogical chart of a family tree

WEB QUIZ
. . . .

Instructions: Try your hand at creating words! Connect the correct root word listed in the inner circle to the word parts listed in the outer circles. You may have to use a root word more than once!

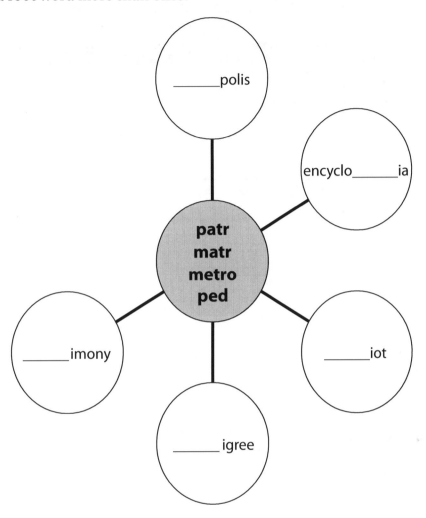

FILL IN THE BLANK
. . . .

Instructions: Use the words in the tables for Lesson 7.2 to complete the sentences below.

1. As an American citizen in the army, some people might consider me to be

   a _____.

2. My family's _____ is very long and rich in history.

3. Mrs. Garcia is the _____ at our private Catholic school.

4. New York City, because of its size, may be described as a

   _____.

LESSON 7.3: FRIEND OR LOVED ONE

Soci comes from Latin and means to unite, be with, or join. *Phil* is Greek and means love. These roots signal words with meanings that describe relationships with others and *phil*, in particular, describes love of someone or something.

Beginning	Root Word	Ending	New Word	Definition
	soci	al	social	having to do with humans interacting in groups; friendly
as	**soci**	ate	associate	to have a relationship with, as a partner, companion, or friend (v); the person associated with (n); joined with others, connected to (adj)
	phil	anthropy	philanthropy	love or goodwill to fellow human beings shown by giving time and money to charity
	phil	harmonic	philharmonic	literally, "love of harmony"; a symphony orchestra
	phil	osophy	philosophy	"love of wisdom"; a branch of learning that deals with the problems of human existence and knowledge

SYNONYM SEARCH

Instructions: Sort through the words and phrases in the word bank to find synonyms for the vocabulary words listed below. Write the synonyms on the lines next to the words they correspond with. Be careful—some of the words in the word bank will not be used!

Word Bank: love of books, symphony orchestra, enemy, love of wisdom, brother, friendly, charity, organization, partner

1. philanthropy _____

2. associate _____

3. philosophy _____

4. philharmonic _____

5. social _____

GUESS THE MEANING

Instructions: For each word below, guess its meaning, writing your guess in the second column. Then, look up the word in a dictionary and write the real meaning in the third column.

word	I think it means . . .	It really means . . .
society		
socialize		
social worker		
philanthropist		
bibliophile		

LESSON 7.4: BIRTH

The roots for birth and the newly born are *par*, *nai*, *nat*, and *gen*.

Beginning	Root Word	Ending	New Word	Definition
	par	ent	parent	mother, father, or ancestor
re	**nai**	ssance	renaissance	rebirth, as in arts and learning in Europe
	nat	ure	nature	the essential or inborn qualities of something or someone
	nat	ive	native	a person born in and living in a certain geographical area
in	**nat**	e	innate	describes abilities or traits that one has from birth
	gen	der	gender	a grammatical classification describing how nouns are grouped (usually, masculine, feminine, and neuter); it also refers to the fact of being male or female
re	**gen**	erate	regenerate	to replace or recreate that which has been destroyed or damaged (like geckos, which regenerate lost limbs)
	gen	eration	generation	a bringing into being, procreation, production; the period of about 30 years between the birth of one generation and the next
	gen	etic	genetic	pertaining to the genes that make us who we are

PICK THE WORD

Instructions: Circle the best word or phrase that completes each sentence.

1. My grandparents' *(genetics, generation, gender)* is called the Baby Boomers.

2. When we go hiking, my uncle Tony says to be "one with *(native, natural, nature)*."

3. Jay, my cousin, has a rare *(genetic, gender, generation)* disorder that causes him to use a wheelchair.

4. The arts have enjoyed a *(reworking, generation, renaissance)* in our town, with many new art shows and festivals occurring this summer.

WEB QUIZ

Instructions: Try your hand at creating words! Connect the correct root word listed in the inner circle to the word parts listed in the outer circles. You may have to use a root word more than once!

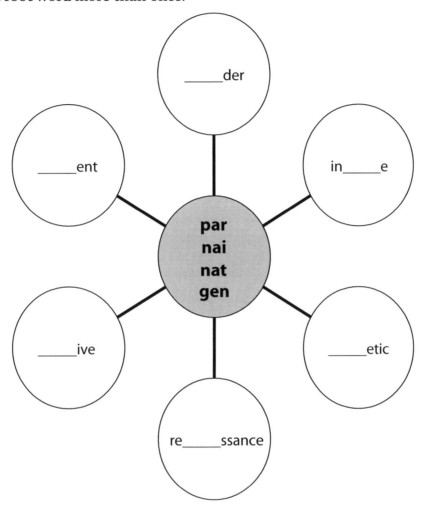

LESSON 7.5: HOME

The roots for home are *dom*, *domin* (Latin), and *eco* (Greek). *Cam and cham* are Greek for room. *Dom* comes from the Latin words for house, landed property, and rulership.

Beginning	Root Word	Ending	New Word	Definition
	dom	estic	domestic	pertaining to a household
	eco	nomics	economics	social science dealing with making, selling, and consuming goods
	eco	system	ecosystem	system made up of a community and its relationships
	cam	era	camera	room or chamber; a device for taking pictures
	cham	ber	chamber	vaulted room with an arched roof

MATCHING

Instructions: Match the root words to their meanings.

Words
1. chamber
2. ecosystem
3. economics
4. domestic

Definitions
a. creation, sale, and use of goods
b. vaulted room
c. a community and its relationships
d. household

FILL IN THE BLANK

Instructions: Use the words for Lesson 7.5 to complete the sentences below.

1. A private room or space in a house is sometimes called a _____.

2. My mom went to the grocery store to buy _____ products for the house.

3. After the graduation ceremony, my teacher took a picture of the class with her _____.

4. The _____ of a country often influence its political power.

LESSON 7.6: FIRE AND BURN

FLAMINGO FLAMENCO

FIRE

The roots for fire are *volcan*, *flam*, *ign*, and *pyr*.

Beginning	Root Word	Ending	New Word	Definition
	volcan	o	volcano	burning mountain, such as Mt. Etna in Sicily
	flam	e	flame	a blazing fire, a tongue of light from a fire
in	**flam**	e	inflame	to set on fire
	flam	ingo	flamingo	tropical bird with pink to scarlet feathers
	ign	ition	ignition	a firing or sparking of the explosive mixture of fuel and air in an engine
	pyr	otechnics	pyrotechnics	brilliant display of fireworks in shows

BURN

Roots that mean burning are *caust* (Greek) and *toast*.

Beginning	Root Word	Ending	New Word	Definition
	caust	ic	caustic	capable of causing a burn in the flesh, as lye
	toast		toast	to turn brown by heat; bread browned and crisped by heat

WEB QUIZ

Instructions: Try your hand at creating words! Connect the correct root word listed in the inner circle to the word parts listed in the outer circles. You may have to use a root word more than once!

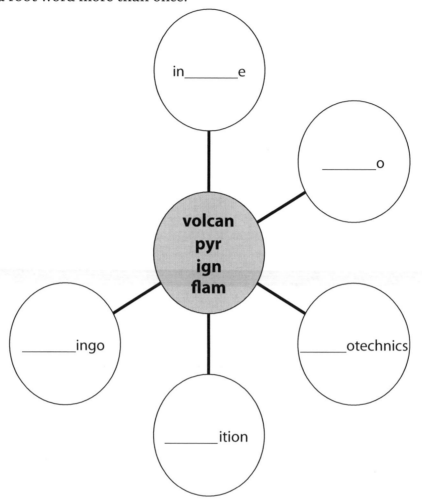

WORD SPLITS

Instructions: The makers of a new dictionary want to break up some words into their word parts for their new edition, but need your help! Can you divide the following words into their word parts? Think carefully—a few words may be new to you!

1. inflame: _____ + _____ + _____

2. ignition: _____ + _____

3. toasty: _____ + _____

4. flammable: _____ + _____

5. volcanic: _____ + _____

LESSON 7.7: COOK

The roots for cooking are *coc*, *cui*, *cot*, and *roti*. These three roots determine when a word's meaning pertains to the act of cooking or something used in the cooking process, or even a cooked item itself.

Beginning	Root Word	Ending	New Word	Definition
con	**coc**	tion	concoction	ingredients put together and cooked
pre	**coc**	ious	precocious	prematurely developed or matured
bis	**cui**	t	biscuit	baked twice; a cookie, wafer, or quick bread
terra	**cot**	ta	terra cotta	brownish-red, unglazed earthenware
ri	**cot**	ta	ricotta	"recooked"; a soft Italian cheese made from whey
	roti	sserie	rotisserie	a rotating grill for roasting or cooking

MATCHING

Instructions: Match the root words to their meanings.

Words
1. concoction
2. biscuit
3. rotisserie
4. ricotta

Definitions
a. recooked
b. ingredients put together
c. grill for cooking
d. baked twice

WORD MATH

Instructions: Read the instructions in the box in order to create a new word by changing the word before it. Use the clues at the bottom of the box to help you create the new words.

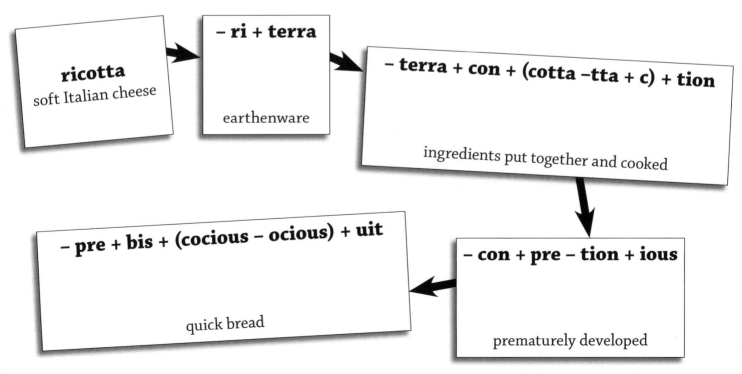

ricotta
soft Italian cheese

– ri + terra

earthenware

– terra + con + (cotta –tta + c) + tion

ingredients put together and cooked

– con + pre – tion + ious

prematurely developed

– pre + bis + (cocious – ocious) + uit

quick bread

LESSON 7.8: FIT TO DRINK

The Latin roots signifying drinkable are *pot* and *poi*.

Beginning	Root Word	Ending	New Word	Definition
	pot	able	potable	drinkable, fit to drink
	pot	ion	potion	a medicinal, magical, or poisonous drink
	pot	ent	potent	having authority; strong or rich
	pot	tage	pottage	soup
	poi	son	poison	deadly substance

FILL IN THE BLANK

Instructions: Use the words for Lesson 7.8 to complete the sentences below.

1. The witch in the cartoon made a _____ to kill the prince.

2. The bite of a Black Widow spider contains _____, so you shouldn't play with them.

3. My coffee had a very _____ aroma that reminded me of my grandparents' house.

WHAT DOESN'T BELONG?

Instructions: Choose the word in each line that *does not* mean the same as the first word.

1. **potent**   strong   sour   rich

2. **pottage**   wine   soup   stew

3. **potable**   safe   carryable   drinkable

4. **poison**   deadly substance   harmful chemical   potable material

CHAPTER 7 REVIEW

BACK"WORDS" WEBS

Instructions: Using the definitions provided, fill in each outer circle on the webs below. Then, decide what each set of words has in common, writing the interconnecting theme for each web in the center circle.

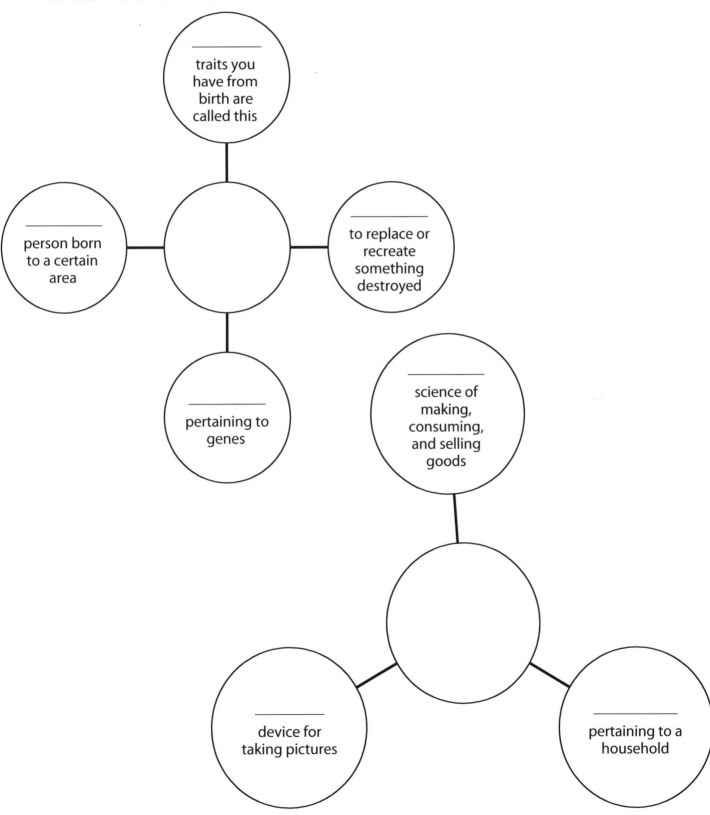

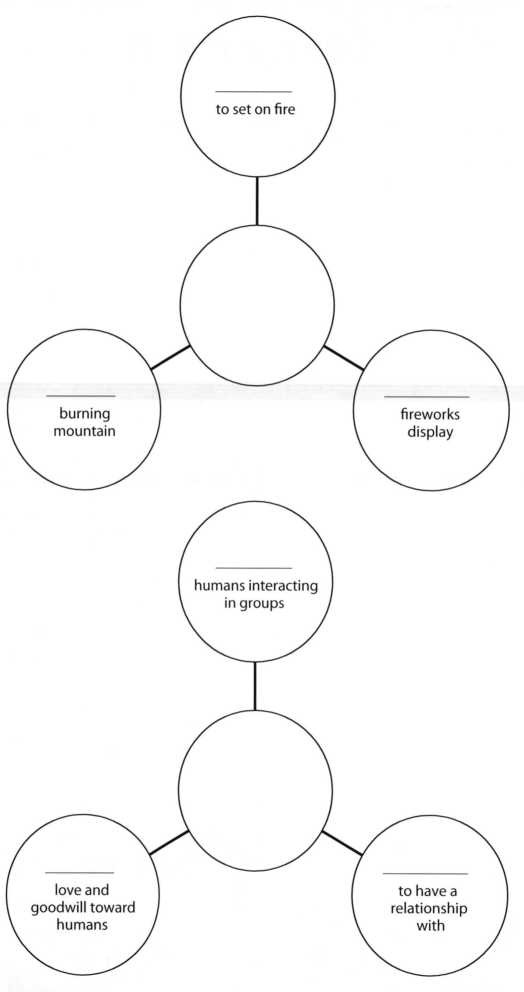

_____
to set on fire

_____
burning
mountain

_____
fireworks
display

_____
humans interacting
in groups

_____
love and
goodwill toward
humans

_____
to have a
relationship
with

CHAPTER 8

Education, Fine Arts, and Sports

The education of children consists not only of formal classes in academic disciplines, such as social studies and mathematics, but also in fine arts and athletics.

Of all the arts enjoyed by the Greek and Roman peoples, drama was one of the most preferred. During the more festive holidays, dramatic competitions were held. Playwrights would submit a play or a series of plays and compete for top honors for the year. Drama was a community event, and Aristotle thought that these plays, tragedies in particular, served the public good because they took away people's stronger emotions and passions, making them more balanced and moderate.

Sports also played a large role in Greek and Roman society. Wrestling was a popular favorite, as was running and jumping. The showy chariot races were also a great crowd-pleaser. For the Greek city-states, the number of competitors sent to the chariot races at the Olympics was a matter of civic pride. Unlike the modern Olympics, only Greek free men could compete.

LESSON 8.1: TEACH/TEACHER AND STUDY

TEACH/TEACHER

Doc, *tut*, and *tui* all come from Latin. *Tut* comes from the Latin for guardian or private teacher. These roots form the foundation of many educational words today and carry additional meanings of the quality of being teachable, learning materials, or the process of learning.

Beginning	Root Word	Ending	New Word	Definition
	doc	tor	doctor	originally, a teacher, advisor, scholar; one who holds a doctorate in healing arts or other field
	doc	ument	document	written or printed information providing information, proof, or a record
	tut	or	tutor	private teacher or guardian
	tui	tion	tuition	fees for instruction at a school or college

STUDY

The Greek suffixes for study are *log* and *logy*. These roots give clues when a word refers to the study of a subject or to the study of something through a specific type of material.

Beginning	Root Word	Ending	New Word	Definition
dia	**log**	ue	dialogue	to converse or speak (v.); a conversation (n.)
mytho	**logy**		mythology	study of myths in a particular culture

MATCHING

Instructions: Match the root words to their meanings.

Words	Definitions
1. log	a. teach
2. doc	b. study
3. logy	
4. tut	
5. tui	

GUESS THE MEANING

Instructions: For each word below, guess its meaning, writing your guess in the second column. Then, look up the word in a dictionary and write the real meaning in the third column.

word	I think it means . . .	It really means . . .
docent		
documentary		
tutorial		
biology		
astrology		

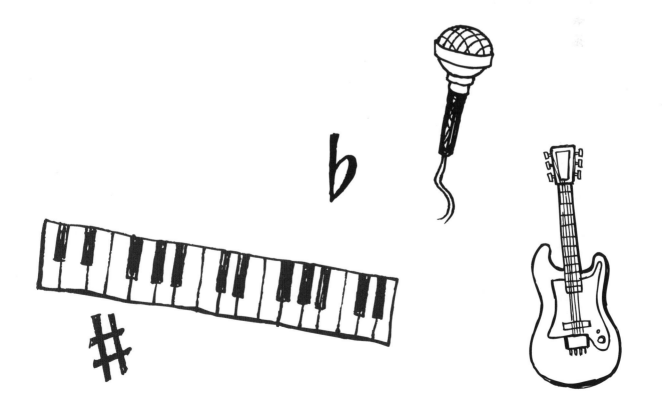

LESSON 8.2: WORD/ROOT WORD AND READ

WORD/ROOT WORD

Verb (Latin) and *Etym* (Greek) describe language or words.

Beginning	Root Word	Ending	New Word	Definition
	verb	al	verbal	relating to words or speech
ad	**verb**		adverb	class of words (part of speech) that modifies verbs, adjectives, and other adverbs
	etym	ology	etymology	study of the origins of words

READ

The root for reading is *leg*, from Latin. This root has two primary uses in English: legal language and the reading and study required in scholarship.

Beginning	Root Word	Ending	New Word	Definition
col	**leg**	e	college	people with certain powers and duties who are engaged in a common pursuit; a school or division at a university offering degrees
	leg	ible	legible	that which can be read

WORD SPLITS

Instructions: The makers of a new dictionary want to break up some words into their word parts for their new edition, but need your help! Can you divide the following words into their word parts? Think carefully—a few words may be new to you!

1. verbal: _____ + _____

2. college: _____ + _____ + _____

3. proverb: _____ + _____

4. illegible: _____ + _____ + _____

5. legend: _____ + _____

FILL IN THE BLANK

Instructions: Use the words for Lesson 8.2 to complete the sentences below.

1. After graduating from high school, I want to study medicine in _____.

2. When I am trying to learn the _____ of a word, I usually look it up in the dictionary.

3. My handwriting is usually clear and _____.

LESSON 8.3: WRITE

Scrib and *scrip* come from Latin and mean to write. *Graph*, *graf*, and *gram* come from Latin and Greek form the foundation of many English literary and drawing words.

Beginning	Root Word	Ending	New Word	Definition
	scrib	ble	scribble	to write carelessly
de	scrib	e	describe	to tell, write about, or picture in words
manu	scrip	t	manuscript	a piece of writing done by hand or the copy of a written work sent to a publisher
pre	scrip	tion	prescription	doctor's orders for medicines to be administered in a certain way for a patient
	graf	fiti	graffiti	scribblings or drawings on a surface or wall
	graph	ics	graphics	illustrations, drawings, or visual arts
	gram	mar	grammar	branch of linguistics that deals with rules of writing and speech in a language
pro	gram		program	list of events in the order they will occur
dia	gram		diagram	a sketch that explains a thing by outlining its parts, relationships, and workings

VOCABULARY IN REAL LIFE

Instructions: Answer the following questions about the vocabulary words for this lesson.

1. In what career(s) might you be required to write someone a prescription?

   _____

2. What are five words that describe your classroom or bedroom? (Think about what these areas look like, smell like, sound like, and feel like to you.)

   _____

   _____

3. On another sheet of paper, draw a diagram of your school playground or common area. Make sure to label each part!

WEB QUIZ

Instructions: Try your hand at creating words! Connect the correct root word listed in the inner circle to the word parts listed in the outer circles. You may have to use a root word more than once!

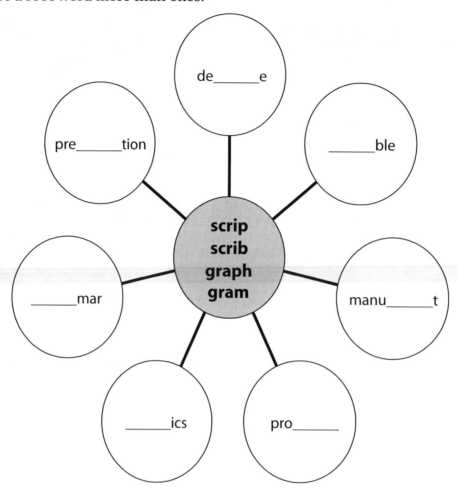

Rockin' Root Words Book 1 © Prufrock Press Inc. • Permission is granted to photocopy or reproduce this page for single classroom use only.

LESSON 8.4: VISUAL ARTS

Art comes from Latin through French to mean skill or talent, as in *artistic*. The roots *sculpt*, *draw*, and *paint* also define types of artistic pursuits.

Prefix	Word Part	Suffix	New Word	Definition
	art		art	the skill applied in music, dancing, painting, and sculpture; also, the human creative ability to make or do things
	art	ist	artist	someone skilled in fine arts
	art	ificial	artificial	man-made; not naturally occurring
	sculpt		sculpt	to form a shape out of a solid object, usually wood or stone, by removing extra material
	paint		paint	a liquid pigment applied to a surface
	draw		draw	to make lines, figures, or pictures on a surface with a pencil, pen, brush, or other tool
	draw	ing	drawing	art of representing something by lines or figures on a surface; the picture or design made

MATCHING

Instructions: Match the words to their definitions.

Words
1. artificial
2. sculptor
3. painting
4. art
5. drawing

Definitions
a. representation of something with lines or figures
b. a piece of art that uses liquid pigment on a surface
c. someone who sculpts
d. not natural
e. creative ability to do or make things

FILL IN THE BLANK

Instructions: Use the words for Lesson 8.4 to complete the sentences below.

1. Many Native American tribes were adept at _____ clay pottery by hand and then hardening it in fire.

2. My friend Sarah is a very good _____, especially when she portrays nature scenes in watercolor.

3. Michelangelo was a famous _____, as were also Shakespeare and Beethoven.

4. In art class we _____ new pictures each week.

LESSON 8.5: MUSIC

The roots for music come from Greek and Latin in the form of *harmon*, *symphon*, *melo*, *ode*, *cant*, and *chant*. These words pertain to songs or the making of music.

Beginning	Root Word	Ending	New Word	Definition
	harmon	y	harmony	a combination of notes played together that sounds pleasing to the ear; any agreement of ideas, feelings, shape, or color that presents a pleasing whole
	symphon	y	symphony	a piece of orchestral music usually with four movements
	melo	dy	melody	a tune or song; pleasing sounds or their arrangement in sequence
	ode		ode	a type of poem written to be sung or a lyric poem addressing a person or thing
	cant	o	canto	a division of certain long poems similar to a chapter of a book
re	**cant**		recant	to sing again; to retract or recall a statement
	chant		chant	simple song; repetitive singing or shouting by a group

FILL IN THE BLANK

Instructions: Use the words for Lesson 8.5 to complete the sentences below.

1. At the football game the crowd began to _____ "Tigers!"

2. My English teacher brought in a _____, which is a division of long poems.

3. During music class the teacher told us all to sing in _____.

4. We sang an _____ to America on the Fourth of July.

5. The _____ of Mariah Carey's new song is soft and beautiful.

6. Because I play cello, I decided to try out for the local kids _____.

WEB QUIZ

Instructions: Try your hand at creating words! Connect the correct root word listed in the inner circle to the word parts listed in the outer circles. You may have to use a root word more than once!

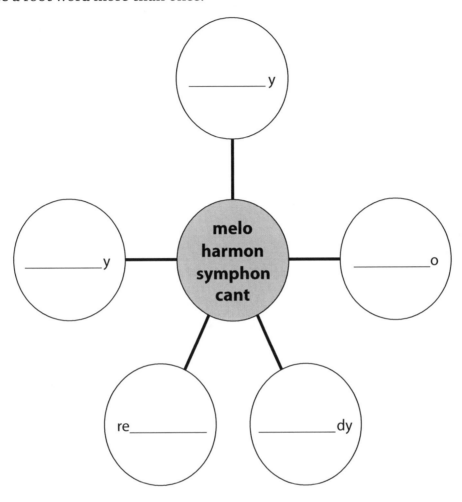

LESSON 8.6: THEATER AND DANCE

THEATER

These five roots determine when a word's meaning refers to plays, theater, or drama. *Theatr* and *scen* come from Greek and Latin; *drama*, *com*, and *trag* come from Greek. These roots form the English words for dramatic situations.

Beginning	Root Word	Ending	New Word	Definition
	theatr	e	theatre	an open place to view a performance (also spelled theater); any place where events take place
	drama		drama	a literary composition of dialogue and action meant to be performed before an audience
	com	edy	comedy	a humorous play or film that often ends better for the characters than the situation in the beginning; a humorous play or film
	trag	edy	tragedy	a play that ends worse than it begins, usually with the death of one or more of the major characters
	scen	e	scene	part of an act in a film or play, specifically, whenever a new character enters or a character exits the stage; the setting of a play, film, opera, or story.

DANCE

The root for dance is *chor* from Greek, and determines when a word's meaning refers to movement in coordination with song or music. This root also defines words that refer to the making of a song or music.

Beginning	Root Word	Ending	New Word	Definition
	chor	al	choral	belonging to a chorus or choir
	chor	eography	choreography	the arrangement or written instructions for a dance, especially ballet
	chor	us	chorus	group of singers who sing together; the music written for them; simultaneous sound by many; also can be a group of dancers who are not the principals (or lead) dancers

MATCHING

Instructions: Match the root words to their meanings.

Words	Definitions
1. tragedy	a. humorous
2. comedy	b. dance instructions
3. drama	c. ends worse than it begins
4. choreography	d. composition of dialogue and action

PICK THE WORD

Instructions: Circle the best word or phrase that completes each sentence.

1. In the school play, I chose to sing in the *(background, chorus, choreography)*.

2. For my birthday, my friend and I saw the very funny new *(drama, tragedy, comedy)* in the theater.

3. The play *Hamlet* ends with many of the characters' deaths, making it a true *(drama, tragedy, comedy)*.

4. The older girls at school act as though their lives are one big *(drama, tragedy, comedy)*, composed of lots of sneaky conversation and unbelievable actions toward one another.

5. I had to turn away during the scary *(chorus, theatre, scene)* in the movie.

6. I love going to the *(chorus, theatre, scene)* with my parents to see the latest musicals.

LESSON 8.7: CONTEST

Athl comes from Greek and *test* from Latin to describe sporting contests. The roots indicate when a word's meaning pertains to a competition or a challenge of some kind.

Beginning	Root Word	Ending	New Word	Definition
	athl	ete	athlete	trained contestant in physical games or sports
tri	**athl**	on	triathlon	endurance contest combining three sports: bicycling, swimming, and running
dec	**athl**	on	decathlon	contest combining 10 different events
	test		test	an examination, experiment, or trial; an event that proves a person's qualities
con	**test**		contest	trial of skill, strength, or other quality

FILL IN THE BLANK

Instructions: Use the words for Lesson 8.7 to complete the sentences below.

1. At the summer Olympics the _____ involves three related

   sporting events.

2. Lebron James is probably the best _____ in professional

   basketball.

3. The marathon was a true _____ of my endurance as a runner.

NUMBERING VOCABULARY

Decathlons and triathlons are not the only sporting events to use this terminology. Go back to Chapter 1 and use the number terms listed there to match up the following "–athlons" with the number of events included in each.

Sport
1. pentathlon
2. biathlon
3. quadrathlon
4. heptathlon

Number of Events
a. two
b. seven
c. five
d. four

Name:_____ Date:_____

LESSON 8.8: STRENGTH

Roots for strength are *fort* (Latin), *val* (Latin), and *dynam* (Greek). *Fort* means "a structure for defense," val means to be well or strong, and dynam means power or strength.

Beginning	Root Word	Ending	New Word	Definition
	fort	e	forte	strong point
	fort	ify	fortify	to make strong or strengthen defenses
pre	**val**	ent	prevalent	widespread; common in many places
equi	**val**	ent	equivalent	equal in strength
	val	ue	value	real worth; purchasing power; precise meaning
	dynam	ic	dynamic	powerful, energetic

WEB QUIZ

Instructions: Try your hand at creating words! Connect the correct root word listed in the inner circle to the word parts listed in the outer circles. You may have to use a root word more than once!

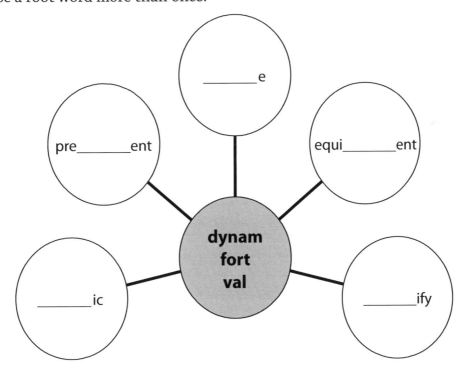

ALL MIXED UP

Instructions: Help! The following word parts were all mixed up in the dictionary. Connect the word parts by drawing lines between the boxes. Then, write the correct words in the lines next to their definitions. Be careful! Some of the connections can be tricky: You only want to find words that match the definitions below.

1. _____: strong point

2. _____: equal in strength

3. _____: strengthen

4. _____: energetic

5. _____: common

6. _____: real worth

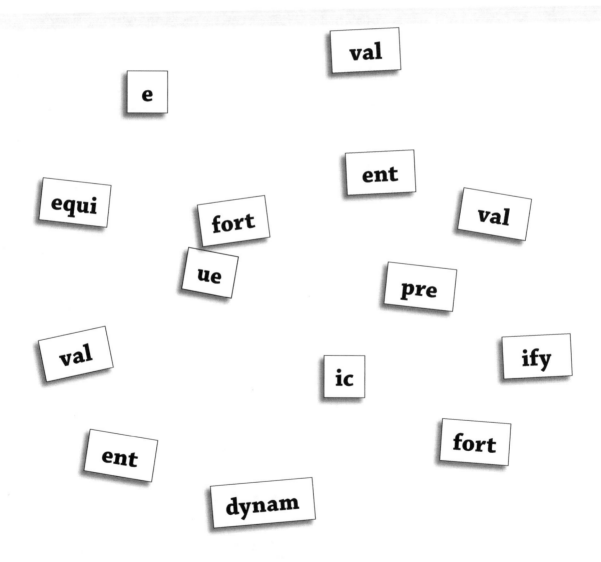

CHAPTER 8 REVIEW

ROOT WORDS PUZZLER

Instructions: Combine the puzzle pieces to build new words. If you'd like, cut the pieces out and paste them on another sheet of paper.

GRAFFITI GURUS

Instructions: Graffiti is an artform practiced both legally and illegally across the U.S. Some cities impose large fines on people caught painting illegal graffiti. With the help of your teacher or parent, visit the website http://www.graffitihurts.org and click on the Learn More link. Explore the information about graffiti, and then write or type a letter to your mayor explaining whether you think your community should ban graffiti. Be sure to include at least three reasons for your decision and use the information you've learned from this website. Try to use the vocabulary words from this chapter in your letter!

_____

_____

_____

_____

_____

_____

_____

_____

_____

_____

_____

_____

_____

_____

_____

_____

_____

_____

CHAPTER 9
Building and Construction

The Romans were masters of building cities, roads, and waterways. The old saying goes "all roads lead to Rome" and, at one time, that was true. The extensive reach of Rome throughout the known world meant that they would need food, water, and transportation, and ways to move a great number of soldiers quickly and efficiently in the case of war. Some of the Roman accounts of the far reaches of their empire are quite amusing, and some of their observations of the natives were off-base, but their maps and written accounts of those regions (like Britain) teach us a lot about the early history of Western Europe.

LESSON 9.1: ROCK OR STONE AND WOOD

ROCK OR STONE

The roots for rock or stone are *pet(r)* from the Greek word for rock and *lith* from the word for stone. These roots find their way in the English language to create words that pertain to something gathered from or related to stone.

Beginning	Root Word	Ending	New Word	Definition
	petr	ify	petrify	to turn into stone; to paralyze with fear
	petr	oleum	petroleum	flammable, liquid hydrocarbon compound found in rocks and used to make fuel oil, paraffin, and gasoline
mega	**lith**		megalith	huge stone used for ancient monuments
meso	**lith**	ic	Mesolithic	brief period of Stone Age between Paleolithic and Neolithic
	lith	osphere	lithosphere	crust and upper mantle of the Earth

WOOD

Xyl(o) derives from the Greek word for wood. When you recognize this root, you can make sense of complicated words like xylograph (a drawing on wood).

Beginning	Root Word	Ending	New Word	Definition
	xylo	phone	xylophone	Wooden musical percussion instrument

MATCHING

Instructions: Match the root words to their meanings.

Words
1. lith
2. xylo
3. petr

Definitions
a. wood
b. rock or stone

FILL IN THE BLANK

Instructions: Use the words for Lesson 9.1 to complete the sentences below.

1. In geography class we learned of the Earth's crust and the

   _____.

2. The price of _____ has increased, therefore gas prices have

   increased.

3. My mom played the _____ when she was a child.

LESSON 9.2: LABOR

The roots for labor are *oper* from Latin and *lab* from Latin through French. These roots give rise to words that define hard work and form the roots of a favorite dog breed, named for the Labrador province of Newfoundland, Canada.

Beginning	Root Word	Ending	New Word	Definition
	oper	ate	operate	to work, act, function; perform surgery
	oper	ation	operation	performance of work or surgical procedure
co	oper	ate	cooperate	to work or act together in harmony
	oper	a	opera	musical drama, usually comic or tragic
	lab	or	labor	work, exertion, or toil; all wage-earning workers collectively; the process of giving birth
	lab	oratory	laboratory	a scientific testing facility
col	lab	orate	collaborate	to work together; to aid and cooperate with an occupying enemy

WHAT DOESN'T BELONG?
. . . .
Instructions: Choose the word in each line that *does not* mean the same as the first word.

1. **operate**   work   function   supply

2. **labor**   shift   toil   exertion

3. **collaborate**   work together   hinder   cooperate

4. **cooperate**   work in harmony act together   play alone

WEB QUIZ

Instructions: Try your hand at creating words! Connect the correct root word listed in the inner circle to the word parts listed in the outer circles. You may have to use a root word more than once!

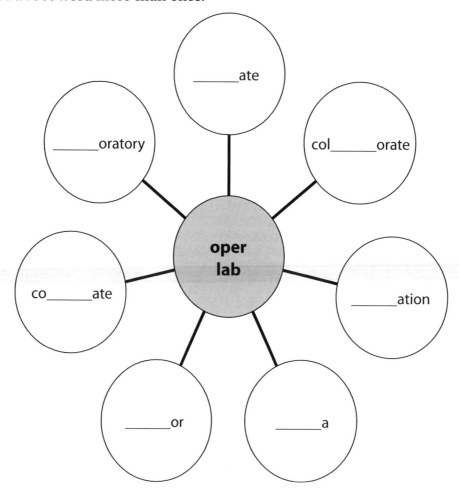

Rockin' Root Words Book 1 © Prufrock Press Inc. • Permission is granted to photocopy or reproduce this page for single classroom use only.

LESSON 9.3: MAKE/DO

Ag comes from the Latin word for to do something or to go, drive, or lead as in agriculture. *Fact/fect* come from the Latin word for to do and express something done. *Fic, feas, feat, fit, feit,* and *fy* are roots that create words for action or possibility.

Beginning	Root Word	Ending	New Word	Definition
	ag	ent	agent	someone working on behalf of someone else
	fact	or	factor	agent, maker, ingredient; anything bringing about a result
af	**fect**	ion	affection	friendly feeling; fond, tender, or warm feeling
unof	**fic**	ial	unofficial	not by, of, or from proper authority
	feas	ible	feasible	able to be done or carried out
	feat	ure	feature	to make a special display of; distinct or outstanding part, quality, or characteristic of something; a special story; a full-length film
de	**feat**		defeat	undo, lose, bring to nothing, frustrate; the fact of being defeated
pro	**fit**		profit	benefit, advantage, gain
for	**feit**		forfeit	to lose something or have it taken away as punishment
magni	**fy**		magnify	to make larger or increase in size

CHANGE IT UP

Instructions: Replace the underlined word or words in each sentence with one of the vocabulary words in the word bank.

Word Bank: forfeit, agent, feasible, profit, factor

1. My mother is a real estate <u>salesperson</u> who sells houses in the city for busy clients.
2. This project is not impossible; instead, it's totally <u>able to be done</u>.
3. One <u>ingredient</u> in solving a math problem is to know the formulas.
4. We hope to make a <u>gain</u> off our concession stand business.
5. I had to <u>give up</u> my allowance this week for starting an argument with my sister.

ALL MIXED UP

Instructions: Help! The following word parts were all mixed up in the dictionary. Connect the word parts by drawing lines between the boxes. Then, write the correct words in the lines next to their definitions. Be careful! Some of the connections can be tricky: You only want to find words that match the definitions below.

1. _____: to increase in size
2. _____: quality or characteristic of something
3. _____: anything bringing about a result
4. _____: without proper authority
5. _____: loss
6. _____: friendly feelings

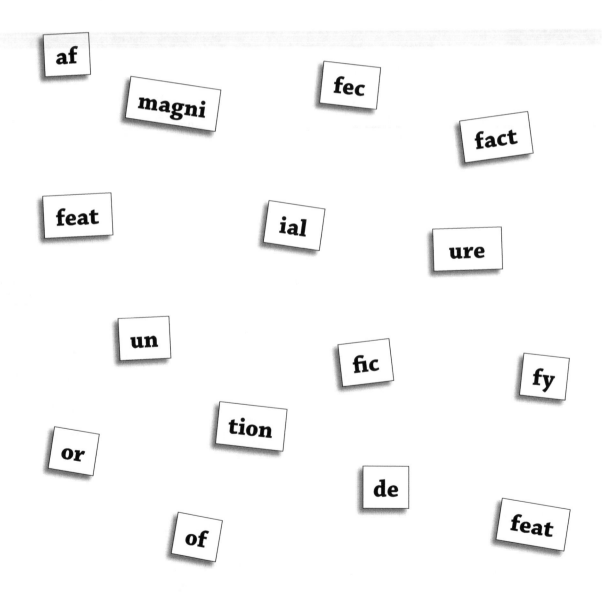

Rockin' Root Words Book 1 © Prufrock Press Inc. • Permission is granted to photocopy or reproduce this page for single classroom use only.

LESSON 9.4: MAKE USE OF

The roots for use are *us* and *ut*. *Sume* is another root that means to make use of something.

Beginning	Root Word	Ending	New Word	Definition
	us	e	use	to put into service, practice, exercise; to make familiar; to take or consume regularly; act of using
dis	**us**	e	disuse	state of not being utilized
ab	**us**	e	abuse	to use wrongly, mistreat, inflict hurt or harm; wrong, bad, harmful, or excessive use
	ut	ilize	utilize	to use, make profitable use of
	ut	ensil	utensil	thing for use, tool, silverware
as	**sume**		assume	to take up, as a duty, office, or role; to seize, take over, take upon oneself; take for granted, suppose; to make believe or pretend to have
con	**sume**		consume	to use up, eat; to destroy, as by fire; to absorb or be overly concerned
re	**sume**		resume	to take up again

WEB QUIZ

Instructions: Try your hand at creating words! Connect the correct root word listed in the inner circle to the word parts listed in the outer circles. You may have to use a root word more than once!

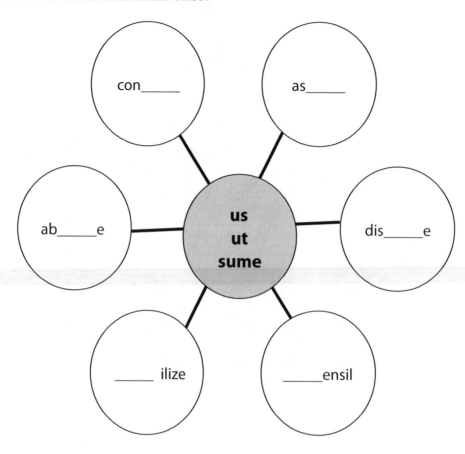

FILL IN THE BLANK

Instructions: Use the words for Lesson 9.4 to complete the sentences below.

1. The coach advised me to play volleyball and _____ my natural

   athletic talents.

2. I threw the newspaper in the fireplace and watched the flames

   _____ the day's headlines.

3. When we go camping, we use metal plates and cups as _____

   for eating.

4. After my broken foot healed, I decided to _____ my daily run.

LESSON 9.5: MELT/POUR/MIX

Latin roots for combine are *fus(e)*, *misc*, and *mix*. These roots are found in many cooking terms, but also in words that describe other situations, such as confusion.

Beginning	Root Word	Ending	New Word	Definition
	fus	e	fuse	to unite by melting together; to join by melting
re	**fus**	e	refuse	to reject, deny, decline; anything thrown away as useless, trash, rubbish
in	**fus**	e	infuse	to put or pour into, instill, impart; to steep or soak, as tea leaves in water
con	**fus**	e	confuse	to throw into disorder, bewilder, mix up
	misc	ellaneous	miscellaneous	varied, mixed, of different kinds; having various qualities or abilities
	mix	ture	mixture	a combination of ingredients; combination or joining of different things or persons
	mix	er	mixer	person doing mixing, or a machine like a blender; a social gathering

MATCHING

Instructions: Match the root words to their meanings.

Words
1. fuse
2. mixer
3. mixture
4. refuse

Definitions
a. combination of ingredients
b. reject or decline
c. join together by melting
d. social gathering

PICK THE WORD

Instructions: Circle the best word or phrase that completes each sentence.

1. To make dye for my art project I first infused or *(dabbed, dropped, soaked)*

   tea leaves in water.

2. The bag of miscellaneous jelly beans contained my favorite *(mixed, same, similar)*

   flavors.

3. The movie plot was so jumbled, I felt really *(excited, appreciative, confused)*

   when I walked out of the theater.

4. I decided I had to accept the offer; it was one I couldn't *(refuse, redo, recreate)*.

5. By *(separating, removing, combining)* the ingredients in the blender, I

   created the best smoothie mixture ever.

LESSON 9.6: BUILD

The Latin root *struct* refers to words for the creation of buildings or ideas.

Beginning	Root Word	Ending	New Word	Definition
recon	**struct**		reconstruct	rebuild or build again
ob	**struct**		obstruct	to block or stop passage through; to hinder
in	**struct**		instruct	to communicate learning; teach, educate
de	**struct**	ion	destruction	demolition, ruin, damage; destroying
con	**struct**	ion	construction	building; an interpretation

WORD SPLITS

Instructions: The makers of a new dictionary want to break up some words into their word parts for their new edition, but need your help! Can you divide the following words into their word parts? Think carefully—a few words may be new to you!

1. obstruct: _____ + _____

2. destruction: _____ + _____ + _____

3. construct: _____ + _____

4. instruction: _____ + _____ + _____

5. reconstruct: _____ + _____

POSITIVE OR NEGATIVE?

Instructions: Choose the words that match each definition below. Then, sort the words into classifications in the Venn diagram, putting the words that have a positive meaning for "build" on the left side and the words that have a negative meaning for "build" on the right side.

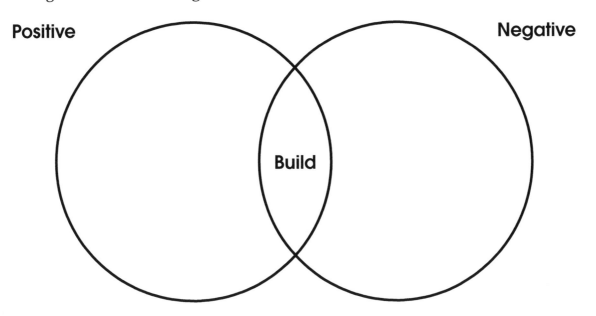

Positive   **Negative**

Build

1. building or interpretation: _____

2. demolition or damage: _____

3. to teach or build up knowledge: _____

4. to block: _____

5. to build again: _____

CHAPTER 9 REVIEW

ROOT WORD PYRAMID

Instructions: You've discovered a rare root word pyramid, but it's falling down! Fill in the missing pieces to the pyramid by completing the information in each block using the word bank. Read each block carefully: Some of the blocks require that you fill in the definitions for your vocabulary words and some require that you add the missing vocabulary word.

Word Bank: feasible, stone, work, laboratory, unofficial, tool, abuse, combination, fuse, build

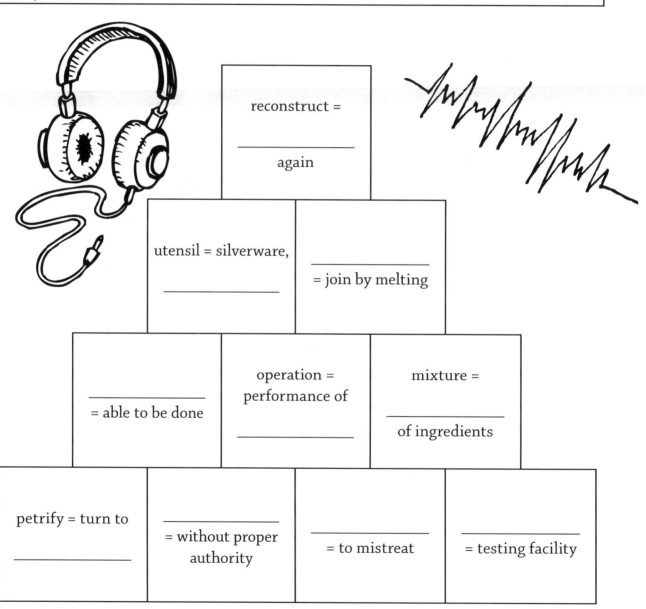

reconstruct = _____ again

utensil = silverware, _____

_____ = join by melting

_____ = able to be done

operation = performance of _____

mixture = _____ of ingredients

petrify = turn to _____

_____ = without proper authority

_____ = to mistreat

_____ = testing facility

CHAPTER 10
Word Endings, or Suffixes

Chapter 10 covers the endings of words, which change parts of speech or the meaning of a root word. We call these endings suffixes.

Suffixes are single letters, syllables, or groups of syllables added after roots or words to make new words or to change the meanings of other words. Suffixes are like prefixes because they are both added to the roots to produce new words. Suffixes are powerful because they can change not only the word's meaning but also its part of speech.

LESSON 10.1: CONCRETE NOUN-FORMING SUFFIXES

The suffixes *er*, *ar*, and *or* signify that someone is or does something. The suffixes *ist*, *ee*, and *eer* form many words for persons sharing hobbies, careers, attitudes, and situations. The suffix *ess* does the same, but specifies female.

Beginning	Suffix	New Word	Definition
climb	**er**	climber	one who climbs, such as a mountaineer
li	**ar**	liar	one who tells lies
burgl	**ar**	burglar	thief; robber of houses
emper	**or**	emperor	one who rules an empire
edit	**or**	editor	someone who edits, selects, or corrects writing before it is published
dent	**ist**	dentist	specialist in the care of teeth
train	**ee**	trainee	person who is being trained, as for a job
devot	**ee**	devotee	one who is devoted to a belief, hobby, celebrity, or to others
engin	**eer**	engineer	person who operates engines or plans, builds, or maintains technical or construction equipment
waitr	**ess**	waitress	female restaurant worker who takes orders and delivers food (the preferred term now for both males and females is "server")

ADDING SUFFIXES

Instructions: The suffixes in this lesson can be used to define many professions. Look at the suffixes above as you think about each of the definitions below. Then, write the correct suffix in each blank to complete the name of the professional who works in each career.

1. someone who creates art is called an art_____

2. someone who manages others is called a manag_____

3. someone who is employed by someone else is called an employ____

4. someone who employs others is called an employ_____

5. someone who mends clothing is called a tail____

WEB QUIZ

Instructions: Try your hand at creating words! Connect the correct suffix listed in the inner circle to the word parts listed in the outer circles. You may have to use a suffix more than once!

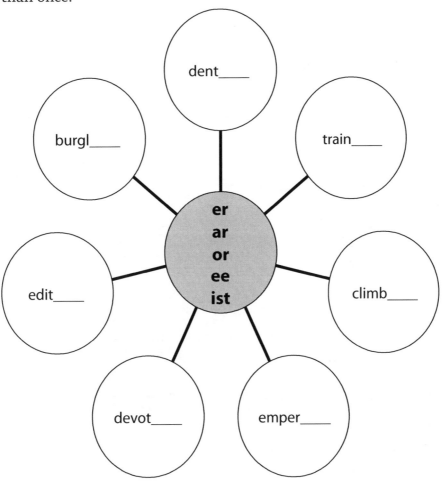

LESSON 10.2: NOUNS-OBJECTS

The suffixes *er, ar,* and *or* also can represent objects. The suffix *ing* refers to materials in total. The suffix *ery* refers to tools or facilities.

Beginning	Suffix	New Word	Definition
toast	**er**	toaster	an electrical gadget for toasting bread
hang	**er**	hanger	device for hanging and storing clothing
coll	**ar**	collar	to set on fire
calend	**ar**	calendar	a fixed system of dividing time in a year into months and days; the chart or table that shows that system
elevat	**or**	elevator	something that raises or lifts up
generat	**or**	generator	engine used to make electricity
cloth	**ing**	clothing	clothes, garments, coverings for the body
floor	**ing**	flooring	material used to build or replace a floor
station	**ery**	stationery	materials used in writing letters (e.g., paper)
machin	**ery**	machinery	combination of machines used for a particular purpose

MAKE A WORD

Instructions: Match the correct beginning word and suffix together to make five words. For example, the root word "floor" and the ending "ing" together make the word "flooring." The beginnings and suffixes will be used only once.

Beginning	Suffix	New Word
elevat	**ery**	
machin	**er**	
cloth	**ar**	
toast	**ing**	
coll	**or**	

FILL IN THE BLANK

Instructions: Use the words for Lesson 10.2 to complete the sentences below.

1. I bought a _____ for my friend so she would remember my birthday.

2. The _____ broke down on our way to the building's fifth floor.

3. We lost all of our power for a week due to the hurricane, but thankfully we had a _____ that allowed us to run an air conditioner.

4. The beautiful _____ had my initials in brown ink on blue paper.

LESSON 10.3: ABSTRACT NOUN-FORMING SUFFIXES

The suffixes *ion*, *ation*, and *ment* combine with numerous Latin roots to indicate action, condition, or the result of an act. The suffix *ity* means quality or amount.

Beginning	Suffix	New Word	Definition
profess	**ion**	profession	accepting belief or faith; occupation
pollut	**ion**	pollution	contamination, corruption, or the act of making something unclean
permiss	**ion**	permission	a permit; allowing or consenting
celebr	**ation**	celebration	a special joyous event; to honor
starv	**ation**	starvation	extreme hunger
instru	**ment**	instrument	means by which something is done; tool, implement; device producing music
orna	**ment**	ornament	something that adorns or decorates, such as jewelry
state	**ment**	statement	an expression of opinion or facts
pur	**ity**	purity	quality of being pure or clean
abil	**ity**	ability	talent, power, or skill to accomplish a task

CHANGE IT UP

Instructions: Replace the underlined word or words in each sentence with one of the vocabulary words in the word bank.

Word Bank: profession, permission, celebration, statement, ability

1. Josiah showed his natural basketball <u>talent</u> when he won the regional dribbling contest.
2. My father's <u>occupation</u> is based in the medical field; he is a physician.
3. The letter contained a concise <u>expression</u> of her opinion that the state should lower the speed limit in school zones.
4. I had to ask my parents' <u>consent</u> to go to the movies with my friend Jackie.
5. The <u>joyous event</u> for my friend's birthday was one to remember: laser tag, pizza, and video games.

WEB QUIZ

Instructions: Try your hand at creating words! Connect the correct suffix listed in the inner circle to the word parts listed in the outer circles. You may have to use a suffix more than once!

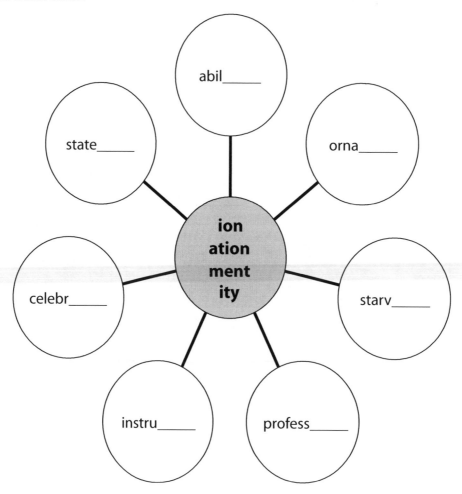

LESSON 10.4: ADJECTIVE-FORMING SUFFIXES

Some adjectives also can be used as nouns, although in this chapter they will be presented only as adjectives. The suffixes *ful* and *ous* show something that is "full of" or "has a quality of," while *less* means a lack of something.

Beginning	Suffix	New Word	Definition
beauti	**ful**	beautiful	very pretty, strikingly attractive, scenic
help	**ful**	helpful	able or willing to help; handy, giving of service
power	**ful**	powerful	very strong; having power
mouth	**ful**	mouthful	as much as the mouth can hold; small amount, especially of food
delici	**ous**	delicious	full of delight; pleasing to the senses, especially taste and smell
fam	**ous**	famous	well-known, renowned, having fame
joy	**ous**	joyous	full of joy, glad, very happy
care	**less**	careless	not cautious and without care; free from worry, unstudied; neglectful, inconsiderate
home	**less**	homeless	without a home to live in
taste	**less**	tasteless	without taste, dull; showing poor taste

FILL IN THE BLANK

Instructions: Use the words for Lesson 10.4 to complete the sentences below.

1. My mother is very kind and has a _____ face.

2. Dry toast is _____. It has no flavor.

3. My cousin's marriage was a _____ occasion. We all loved her new

   husband greatly.

4. I like how _____ I feel when my friends and I volunteer in the library.

ALL MIXED UP

Instructions: Help! The following word parts were all mixed up in the dictionary. Connect the word parts by drawing lines between the boxes. Then, write the correct words in the lines next to their definitions. Be careful! Some of the connections can be tricky: You only want to find words that match the definitions below.

1. _____: without a home

2. _____: pleasing to taste and smell

3. _____: without care

4. _____: strong

5. _____: renowned

6. _____: small amount of food

Rockin' Root Words Book 1 © Prufrock Press Inc. • Permission is granted to photocopy or reproduce this page for single classroom use only.

LESSON 10.5: RESEMBLING OR SIMILAR TO

The suffix *ible* combines with Latin words to mean "similar to," while *able* combines with root words from other origins to mean "resembling." Both roots signify that something is able to be done.

Beginning	Suffix	New Word	Definition
suit	**able**	suitable	appropriate or fit for use
cap	**able**	capable	fit, apt, skillful, having the potential to
read	**able**	readable	fit for or capable of being read; legible
laugh	**able**	laughable	comical, amusing, ridiculous
enjoy	**able**	enjoyable	pleasant; able to give joy
leg	**ible**	legible	that which can be read, especially handwriting; readable
ed	**ible**	edible	something that can be eaten
vis	**ible**	visible	easily seen

WEB QUIZ

Instructions: Try your hand at creating words! Connect the correct suffix listed in the inner circle to the word parts listed in the outer circles. You may have to use a suffix more than once!

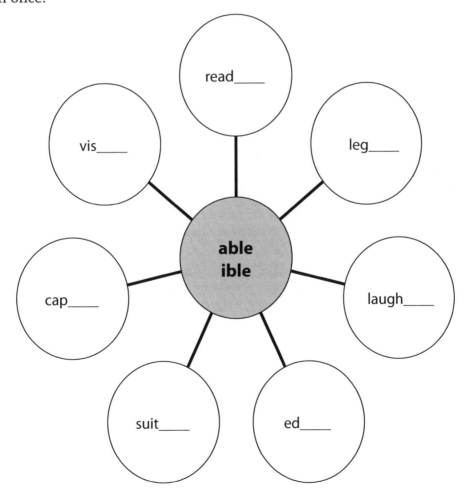

GUESS THE MEANING

Instructions: For each word below, guess its meaning, writing your guess in the second column. Then, look up the word in a dictionary and write the real meaning in the third column.

word	I think it means . . .	It really means . . .
dependable		
flexible		
manageable		
achievable		
audible		

Rockin' Root Words Book 1 © Prufrock Press Inc. • Permission is granted to photocopy or reproduce this page for single classroom use only.

LESSON 10.6: VERB-FORMING SUFFIXES

Common suffixes that make verbs are *fy*, *ize*, *ate*, *en*, and *ed*.

Beginning	Suffix	New Word	Definition
satis	**fy**	satisfy	to make one feel contented or fulfill needs or hopes; to free from doubt or worry
veri	**fy**	verify	to prove true
visual	**ize**	visualize	to see a mental image of
vocal	**ize**	vocalize	to express by voice; to articulate in speech
termin	**ate**	terminate	to finish or end; to dismiss or fire from employment
gradu	**ate**	graduate	to give or take a degree certifying completion of a course of study, to arrange or classify into grades by size, number, or amount
height	**en**	heighten	to raise up or move to a higher position; to increase or intensify, as expectations or hopes
moist	**en**	moisten	to wet or make damp
cross	**ed**	crossed	made a cross; went across
sav	**ed**	saved	helped to survive; rescued; kept, did not discard or throw away

MAKE A WORD

Instructions: Match the correct beginning word and suffix together to make five words. For example, the root word "floor" and the ending "ing" together make the word "flooring." The beginnings and suffixes will be used only once.

Beginning	Suffix	New Word
cross	fy	
gradu	ize	
height	ate	
visual	en	
satis	ed	

SCRAMBLER

Instructions: Unscramble each word listed below. Use the clues to help you decipher the words.

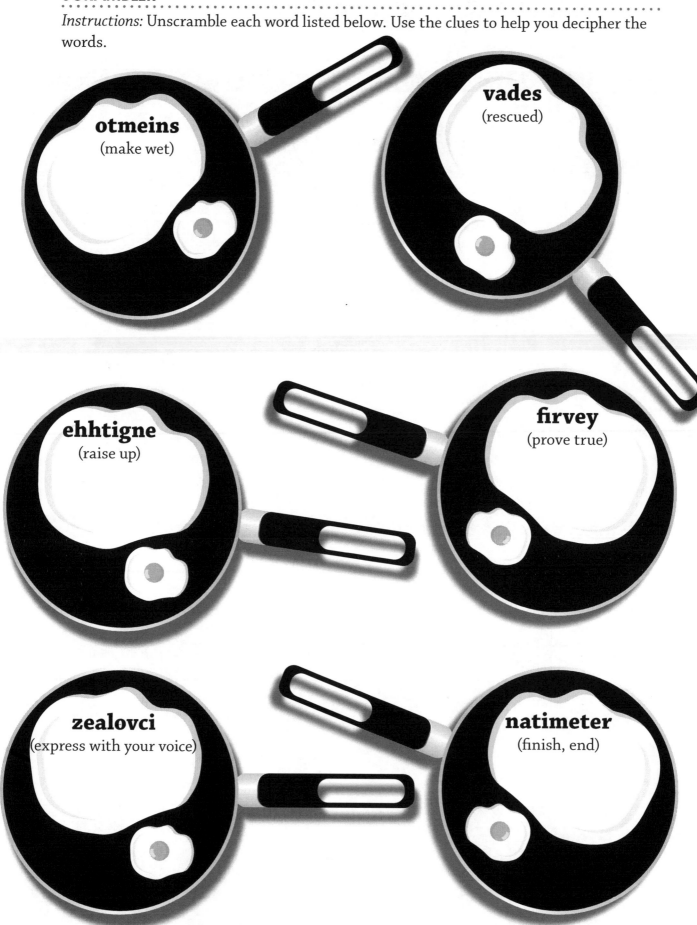

otmeins
(make wet)

vades
(rescued)

ehhtigne
(raise up)

firvey
(prove true)

zealovci
(express with your voice)

natimeter
(finish, end)

Rockin' Root Words Book 1 © Prufrock Press Inc. • Permission is granted to photocopy or reproduce this page for single classroom use only.

LESSON 10.7: ADVERB-FORMING SUFFIXES

Ly is a suffix that shows an adverbial form; this suffix can be added to an adjective or noun to form an adverb.

Beginning	Suffix	New Word	Definition
amiabl	**ly**	amiably	in a friendly, good-natured, or pleasant manner
careless	**ly**	carelessly	in a thoughtless or imprudent way
candid	**ly**	candidly	openly, frankly; in a plainly honest manner
cheerful	**ly**	cheerfully	in a cheerful, joyous, or happy manner
surprising	**ly**	surprisingly	unexpectedly, amazingly
warm	**ly**	warmly	in a warm or friendly way

WORD SPLITS

Instructions: The makers of a new dictionary want to break up some words into their word parts for their new edition, but need your help! Can you divide the following words into their word parts? Think carefully—a few words may be new to you!

1. amiably: _____ + _____

2. warmly: _____ + _____

3. frankly: _____ + _____

4. candidly: _____ + _____

5. beautifully: _____ + _____

FILL IN THE BLANK

Instructions: Use the words for Lesson 10.7 to complete the sentences below.

1. Despite his injury, my crippled dog walked very _____ across the street.

2. I found the pop star's new CD to be _____ enjoyable.

3. My teacher _____ greeted me with "Good morning!" as I walked into the classroom.

CHAPTER 10 REVIEW

WORD QUILT

Instructions: Use the suffixes listed in the center blocks to complete the word quilt. For each suffix, choose four of your vocabulary words from this chapter that use that suffix, writing them in the second strip for each block. Then, write a definition for each word in the third layer of strips. Cut out your blocks and paste them into a square on construction paper (to make your quilt backing). Once you're finished, you'll have a great word quilt to show off your knowledge!

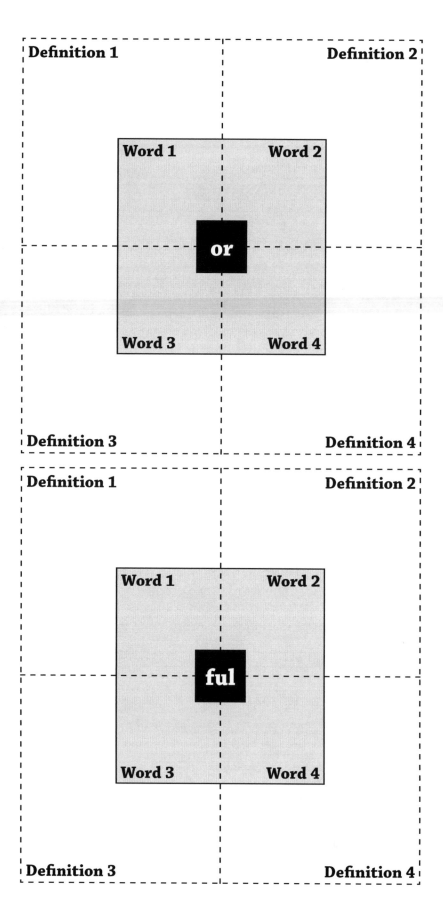

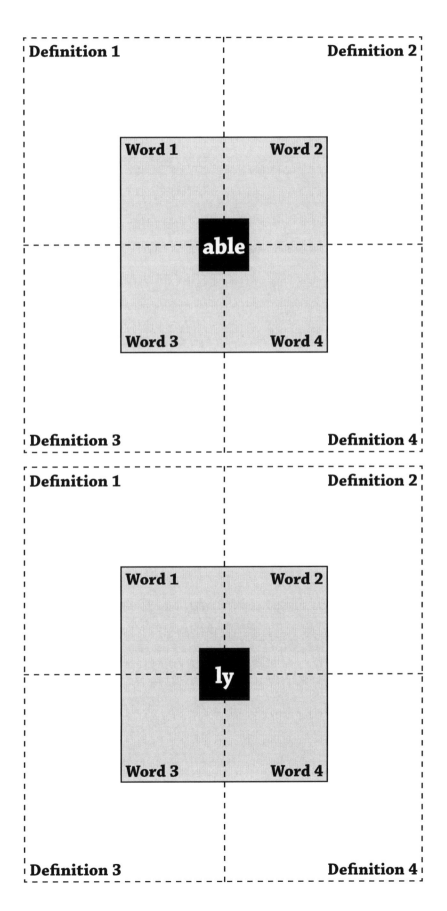

LESSON 1.1

Matching: 1 = d; 2 = c; 3 = b; 4 = a

Fill in the Blank: 1. numbered; 2. numerator; 3. numerous; 4. numerals

LESSON 1.2

Web Quiz 1 (Clockwise from top): hemisphere; semi-circle; semi-trailer; hemi-circle (note that semi-circle and hemi-circle may be switched in order, as both connect to the same word ending)

Web Quiz 2 (Clockwise from top): monorail; unicorn; uniform; unicycle; monolith

LESSON 1.3

Thinking About Vocabulary: 1. Answers will vary, but may include the "Three Little Pigs," or characters like the Three Blind Mice, the Three Musketeers, or the three billy goats Gruff; 2. tripod; 3. Answers will vary.

Web Quiz (Clockwise from top): bicycle; biped; bifocal; duet; dioxide

LESSON 1.4

Matching: 1 = a; 2 = b; 3 = a; 4 = a

Fill in the Blank: 1. quadruplets; 2. quarter; 3. tetrapod; 4. pentagon

LESSON 1.5

More or Less?: 1. more than; 2. less than; 3. less than

Web Quiz (Clockwise from top): octopus; septet; octave; hexagon; September

LESSON 1.6

Make New Words: nonagenarian, nonet, decimeter, decathlon, and decameter

Fill in the Blank: 1. decade; 2. decimal; 3. nonagon

LESSON 1.7

Matching: 1. b; 2. b; 3. a

All Mixed Up: 1. century; 2. kilometer; 3. millipede; 4. centimeter; 5. kilogram

LESSON 1.8

What Doesn't Belong: 1. first; 2. secondary; 3. reptile; 4. finished product; 5. final draft

Fill in the Blank: 1. ultimatum; 2. primate; 3. archives; 4. prototype

CHAPTER 1 REVIEW

Word Bubbles: 1. numerous; 2. duel; 3. sextuplets; 4. archives; 5. hemisphere; 6. quartet; 7. millimeter; 8. uniform; 9. octagon; 10. monolith

LESSON 2.1

Word Splits: 1. amphi + theater; 2. iso + metric; 3. equa + l; 4. equa + tion; 5. iso + tope

Make a Word: isosceles, equator, equilateral, equinox, amphibian, and amphora

LESSON 2.2

Change It Up: 1. plus; 2. multiplied; 3. Holocaust; 4. copious; 5. panoramic; 6. polygons

Web Quiz (Clockwise from top): copious; polygon; hologram; multiplex; multiply

LESSON 2.3

Fill in the Blank: 1. diminish; 2. microscope; 3. miniature; 4. minimum; 5. microphone

Web Quiz (Clockwise from top): microscope; minimize; miniskirt; minimum; microphone; miniature

LESSON 2.4

The Great Divide: Left side: magnificent, magnate, maximum; Right side: maximize, magnify

Adding Suffixes: Answers may vary, but should include definitions along the lines of the following: 1. to make real; 2. to give more energy; 3. to make legal; 4. to make something seen or to see something; 5. to make something shorter or a summary

LESSON 2.5

Matching: 1. b; 2. a.; 3. a; 4. b; 5. a; 6. b

Fill in the Blank: 1. altitude; 2. basement; 3. bassoon; 4. acrobat; 5. longitude; 6. brevity

CHAPTER 2 REVIEW

Word Jumble: 1. polygon; 2. equal; 3. maximum; 4. plural; 5. holocaust; 6. minimum; 7. amphitheater; 8. acrobat; 9. bassoon; 10. isosceles; Jumbled word: cornucopia

LESSON 3.1

Thinking About Vocabulary: 1. Answers will vary, but may include fairy tales like Cinderella (with the clock striking midnight) and Sleeping Beauty (who must sleep for 100 years); 2. chronic; 3. Answers will vary, but will include activities that require a tempo like running or dancing.

Web Quiz (Clockwise from top): temporary; chronology; tempo; chronicle; chronic

LESSON 3.2

Fill in the Blank: 1. postwar; 2. predict; 3. second; 4. antemeridian; 5. premature

Web Quiz (Clockwise from top): premature; secondary; postwar; precaution; prefix; postscript

LESSON 3.3

Matching: 1. b; 2. a.; 3. c; 4. b; 5. c

Pick the Word: 1. daily; 2. night; 3. journey; 4. equal

LESSON 3.4

Make a Word: annual, anniversary, lunar, lunatic, Monday, month, and monthly

Fill in the Blank: 1. perennial; 2. monthly; 3. lunatic; 4. anniversary; 5. centennial

CHAPTER 3 REVIEW

The Word Clock: 1. chronology; 2. lunar; 3. journalism; 4. dial; 5. annual; 6. postscript; 7. horoscope; 8. precaution; 9. nocturnal; 10. temporary; 11. prefix; 12. perennial

My Chronology: Answers will vary. Make sure students include at least five events and put them in chronological order.

LESSON 4.1

Word Splits: 1. loc + ation; 2. al + loc + ate; 3. top + ography l; 4. dis + loc + ate; 5. re + loc + ate; 6. u + top + ia

Web Quiz (Clockwise from top): topic, local, location, topiary, locomotive

LESSON 4.2

Synonym Search: 1. manager; 2. extra; 3. inscription; 4. criminal; 5. surface

Web Quiz (Clockwise from top): overalls, episode, supervisor, outlet, epicenter, superficial

LESSON 4.3

Fill in the Blank: 1. hypothesis; 2. suburbs; 3. underground; 4. hypodermic

Thinking About Vocabulary: Answers will vary, but may include: subdivision, substance,

subscription, submarine, and submit; and underwear, underhand, underarm, underline, and underneath.

LESSON 4.4

Make a Word: The words are: encourage, embroider, eject, incline, introduce, eccentric, and exit.

Outside or Inside?: 1. insèct; 2. embassy; 3. expel; 4. enthusiastic; 5. exhale; 6. eject; 7. index; 8. enclose; The words inside the circle should be: insect, embassy, enthusiastic, index, and enclose; the words outside the circle should be: expel, exhale, and eject.

LESSON 4.5

Thinking About Vocabulary: Answers will vary, but may include: international, internet, interact, and interrupt; and telephone, telethon, telemarket, and teleport.

Fill in the Blank: 1. approximate; 2. interstate; 3. internal; 4. ultraviolet; 5. extragalactic

LESSON 4.6

Matching: 1. d; 2. c; 3. a; 4. b

Pick the Word: 1. high; 2. center; 3. acropolis; 4. center

LESSON 4.7

Analogies: 1. circus; 2. parallel; 3. paragraph

Web Quiz (Clockwise from top): parallel, periscope, circus, perimeter, parasite, circuit

LESSON 4.8

Matching: 1. b; 2. a; 3. b

Scrambler: The unscrambled words are: adverb, abrasion, apostrophe, adhere, admire, apology, abnormal

LESSON 4.9

Web Quiz (Clockwise from top): depress, transform, diagram, deplane, catalog, translate

What Doesn't Belong?: 1. paragraph; 2. lift up; 3. stay the same; 4. artifact; 5. to fall

LESSON 4.10

Guess the Meaning: Answers will vary. Check your class dictionary or an online dictionary of your preference for the exact meanings.

Web Quiz (Clockwise from top): react, reverse, anagram, reflect, relate, analogy

CHAPTER 4 REVIEW

Root Words Mad Lib: Some answers will vary. Students should have the following vocabulary words correctly noted in the following blanks: 3. overflow; 4. location; 5. exit; 6. suburb; 7. interstate; 8. underground; 9. abnormal; 10. reverse; 11. incline; 12. transform; 15. locomotive; 16. acropolis; 19. circus; 20. concentric; 22. catapult

LESSON 5.1

Web Quiz (Clockwise from top): facial, deform, conform, figurine, preface, disfigure
Fill in the Blank: 1. figure; 2. facial; 3. preface; 4. conform; 5. disfigured; 6. uniform

LESSON 5.2

Matching: 1. a; 2. a; 3. b; 4. a
Pick the Word: 1. plates; 2. orthopedic; 3. plain; 4. orthodontist; 5. airplane

LESSON 5.3

Web Quiz (Clockwise from top): oval, rotunda, roundabout, rotation, ovoid
Picturing Vocabulary: 1. Answers will vary, but may include: ball, wheel, bubble gum ball, or bubble; 2. Answers will vary, but may include: bicycle wheels, car wheels, merry-go-rounds, or windmills; 3. Check student pictures to make sure they are of your state capitol and not another building. Students may need assistance with this task.

LESSON 5.4

Fill in the Blank: 1. chrysanthemum; 2. album; 3. Argentina
Make a Word: albatross, chrysalis, chrysanthemum, and Argentina

LESSON 5.5

Matching: 1. d; 2. c; 3. a; 4. b
Scrambler: The unscrambled words are: ruby, cyanide, rubella, rhododendron, and chlorophyll

LESSON 5.6

Analogies: 1. eulogy; 2. dyslexia; 3. differ; 4. disaster; 5. bonus
Thinking About Vocabulary: 1. misfortune; 2. Answers will vary but should be good or advantageous reasons for being a child; 3. Answers will vary. If a natural disaster has occurred recently in your area or is receiving widespread attention (such as the 2010 earthquake in Haiti), you may consider having your students write to these victims. If you wish, you can send your students' letters to the Red Cross for distribution.

LESSON 5.7

Web Quiz (Clockwise from top): alibi, facsimile, alien, similar, heterogeneous, homophone
True or False: 1. F; 2. T; 3. T; 4. T; 5. T; 6. F

CHAPTER 5 REVIEW

Crossword Puzzle: Across: 3. facial; 5. figure; 7. homonym; 9. alibi; 10. cyanide; 13. orthopedics; 14. beneficial; 16. albatross; 17. simulator. Down: 1. plain; 2. deform; 4. chrysalis; 6. ruby; 8. malformed; 11. disturb; 12. roundabout; 15. ovoid

LESSON 6.1

Synonym Search: 1. group; 2. disagreement; 3. specialized tissue; 4. natural; 5. fearless
Word Math: discord, concord, cordial, cardiac

LESSON 6.2

Matching: 1. d; 2. c; 3. a; 4. b; 5. c; 6. c
Fill in the Blank: 1. dentures; 2. optician; 3. cape; 4. oral

LESSON 6.3

Pick the Word: 1. capture; 2. manager; 3. chiropractor; 4. manicures; 5. digital
Web Quiz (Clockwise from top): chiropractor, manage, manual, capture, manicure

LESSON 6.4

Word Splits: 1. mo + ped; 2. pod + ium; 3. platy + pus; 4. octo + pus; 5. ex + ped + ition; 6. anti + pod + es
Word Math: pedicure, expedition, pedestrian, podium

LESSON 6.5

Fill in the Blank: 1. survive; 2. biology; 3. zoology; 4. mortal

Web Quiz (Clockwise from top): biology, vital, zoology, biography, vitamin

LESSON 6.6

Matching: 1. d; 2. c; 3. a; 4. b

Change It Up: 1. sarcophagus; 2. corporation; 3. carnations; 4. carnivores; 5. sarcasm

LESSON 6.7

Web Quiz (Clockwise from top): invisible, periscope, video, visual, evidence, microscope

All Mixed Up: 1. telescope; 2. evidence; 3. invisible; 4. microscope; 5. provide; 6. visual

LESSON 6.8

Telephone Call: auditorium, audience, microphone, monotone, saxophone, tone, telephone

Web Quiz (Clockwise from top): microphone, audience, tone, auditorium, saxophone, sonogram, monotone

LESSON 6.9

Matching: 1. b; 2. a; 3. d; 4. c

Fill in the Blank: 1. contact; 2. tangible; 3. tangent; 4. tact

LESSON 6.10

Pick the Word: 1. nonsense; 2. sentence; 3. sensitive

Guess the Meaning: Answers will vary. Check your class dictionary or an online dictionary of your preference for the exact meanings.

CHAPTER 6 REVIEW

A Matter of Life and Death: Answers will vary. Make sure students use each of the vocabulary words in the word bank in their story and use them correctly. Also make sure that students correctly grasp the difference between mortal and immortal when they describe their characters.

LESSON 7.1

Matching: 1. c; 2. b; 3. a

Change It Up: 1. autograph; 2. feminine; 3. anthropology; 4. autobiography

LESSON 7.2

Web Quiz (Clockwise from top): metropolis, encyclopedia, patriot, pedigree, matrimony

Fill in the Blank: 1. patriot; 2. pedigree; 3. matron; 4. metropolis

LESSON 7.3

Synonym Search: 1. charity; 2. partner; 3. love of wisdom; 4. symphony orchestra; 5. friendly

Guess the Meaning: Answers will vary. Check your class dictionary or an online dictionary of your preference for the exact meanings.

LESSON 7.4

Pick the Word: 1. generation; 2. nature; 3. genetic; 4. renaissance

Web Quiz (Clockwise from top): gender, innate, genetic, renaissance, native, parent

LESSON 7.5

Matching: 1. b; 2. c; 3. a; 4. d

Fill in the Blank: 1. chamber; 2. domestic; 3. camera; 4. economics

LESSON 7.6

Web Quiz (Clockwise from top): inflame, volcano, pyrotechnics, ignition, flamingo

Word Splits: 1. in + flam + e; 2. ign + ition; 3. toast + y; 4. flam + mable; 5. volcan + ic

LESSON 7.7

Matching: 1. b; 2. d; 3. c; 4. a

Word Math: terra cotta, concoction, precocious, biscuit

LESSON 7.8

Fill in the Blank: 1. potion or poison; 2. poison; 3. potent

What Doesn't Belong?: 1. sour; 2. wine; 3. carryable; 4. potable material

CHAPTER 7 REVIEW

Back"Words" Webs: Answers are listed by the "themes" for each web. Birth: innate, regenerate, genetics, native; Home: economics, domestic, camera; Fire: inflame, pyrotechnics, volcano; Friends/Loved Ones: social, associate, philanthropy

LESSON 8.1

Matching: 1. b; 2. a; 3. b; 4. a; 5. a

Guess the Meaning: Answers will vary. Check your class dictionary or an online dictionary of your preference for the exact meanings.

LESSON 8.2

Word Splits: 1. verb + al; 2. col + leg + e; 3. pro + verb; 4. il + leg + ible; 5. leg + end

Fill in the Blank: 1. college; 2. etymology; 3. legible

LESSON 8.3

Vocabulary in Real Life: 1. Answers will vary, but should include a health profession like doctor, nurse, veterinarian, or dentist; 2. Answers will vary; 3. Answers will vary, but make sure each part is labeled appropriately.

Web Quiz (Clockwise from top): describe, scribble, manuscript, program, graphics, grammar, prescription

LESSON 8.4

Matching: 1. d; 2. c; 3. b; 4. e; 5. a

Fill in the Blank: 1. sculpting; 2. painter; 3. artist; 4. draw

LESSON 8.5

Fill in the Blank: 1. chant; 2. canto; 3. harmony; 4. ode; 5. melody; 6. symphony

Web Quiz (Clockwise from top): harmony, canto, melody, recant, symphony (note that harmony and symphony may be switched in order, as both connect to the same word ending)

LESSON 8.6

Matching: 1. c; 2. a; 3. d; 4. b

Pick the Word: 1. chorus; 2. comedy; 3. tragedy; 4. drama; 5. scene; 6. theatre

LESSON 8.7

Fill in the Blank: 1. triathlon; 2. athlete; 3. test

Numbering Vocabulary: 1. c; 2. a; 3. d; 4. b

LESSON 8.8

Web Quiz (Clockwise from top): forte, equivalent, fortify, dynamic, prevalent

All Mixed Up: 1. forte; 2. equivalent; 3. fortify; 4. dynamic; 5. prevalent; 6. value

CHAPTER 8 REVIEW

Root Words Puzzler: The words are: document, mythology, etymology, graffiti, artificial, recant, choral, contest, fortify, and comedy.

Graffiti Gurus: Answers will vary. Make sure students include three reasons for their decision and include correct information from the website.

LESSON 9.1

Matching: 1. b; 2. a; 3. b

Fill in the Blank: 1. lithosphere; 2. petroleum; 3. xylophone

LESSON 9.2

What Doesn't Belong?: supply, shift, hinder, play alone

Web Quiz (Clockwise from top): operate, collaborate, operation, opera, labor, cooperate, laboratory

LESSON 9.3

Change It Up: 1. agent; 2. feasible; 3. factor; 4. profit; 5. forfeit

All Mixed Up: 1. magnify; 2. feature; 3. factor; 4. unofficial; 5. defeat; 6. affection

LESSON 9.4

Web Quiz (Clockwise from top): assume, disuse, utensil, utilize, abuse, consume

Fill in the Blank: 1. use or utilize; 2. consume; 3. utensils; 4. resume

LESSON 9.5

Matching: 1. c; 2. d; 3. a; 4. b

Pick the Word: 1. soaked; 2. mixed; 3. confused; 4. refuse; 5. combining

LESSON 9.6

Word Splits: 1. ob + struct; 2. de + struct + ion; 3. con + struct; 4. in + struct + ion; 5. recon + struct

Positive or Negative?: 1. construction; 2. destruction; 3. instruct; 4. obstruct; 5. reconstruct. Positive words are construction, instruct, and reconstruct; negative words are destruction and obstruct

CHAPTER 9 REVIEW

Root Word Pyramid: Top Row: build; Second Row (left to right): tool, fuse; Third Row (left to right):

feasible, work, combination; Bottom Row (left to right): stone, unofficial, abuse, laboratory

LESSON 10.1
Adding Suffixes: 1. artist; 2. manager; 3. employee; 4. employer; 5. tailor

Web Quiz (Clockwise from top): dentist, trainee or trainer, climber, emperor, devotee, editor, burglar

LESSON 10.2
Make a Word: elevator, machinery, clothing, toaster, collar

Fill in the Blank: 1. calendar; 2. elevator; 3. generator; 4. stationery

LESSON 10.3
Change It Up: 1. ability; 2. profession; 3. statement; 4. permission; 5. celebration

Web Quiz (Clockwise from top): ability, ornament, starvation, profession, instrument, celebration, statement

LESSON 10.4
Fill in the Blank: 1. beautiful; 2. tasteless; 3. joyous; 4. helpful

All Mixed Up: 1. homeless; 2. delicious; 3. careless; 4. powerful; 5. famous; 6. mouthful

LESSON 10.5
Web Quiz (Clockwise from top): readable, legible, laughable, edible, suitable, capable, visible

Guess the Meaning: Answers will vary. Check your class dictionary or an online dictionary of your preference for the exact meanings.

LESSON 10.6
Make a Word: crossed, graduate, heighten, visualize, satisfy

Scrambler: moisten; saved; heighten; verify; vocalize; terminate

LESSON 10.7
Word Splits: 1. amiab + ly; 2. warm + ly; 3. frank + ly; 4. candid + ly; 5. beautiful + ly

Fill in the Blank: 1. carelessly; 2. surprisingly; 3. cheerfully, amiably, or warmly

CHAPTER 10 REVIEW
Word Quilt: Answers will vary, but check students' definitions and word lists against the chapter information. Teachers should make photocopies of these pages so that students can fill in the quilt blocks and paste them on another piece of paper.

REFERENCES

Farstrup, A. E., & Samuels, S. J. (Eds.). (2008). *What research has to say about vocabulary instruction*. Washington, D.C.: International Reading Association

Green, T. M. (1994). *The Greek and Latin roots of English*. Lanham, MD: Rowman and Littlefield.

Thompson, M. C. (2002). Vocabulary and grammar: Critical content for critical thinking. *The Journal of Secondary Gifted Education, 13*(2), 60–66.

ABOUT THE AUTHORS

Manisha Shelley Kaura is a high school senior from the Detroit area. It is her love for and curiosity of this beautiful English language that has carried her through this rather daunting project over the last 8 years. She is a Beatles maniac and loves Indian dance. In the fall of 2010, she will join a 6-year medical program specializing in pediatric neurology.

S. R. Kaura, M.D., is a family physician in private practice in the Detroit metro area. He is the author of two books on preventive medicine, *The Nibbler's Diet* and *Understanding and Preventing Cancer*. He has a special interest in historical linguistics.

Common Core State Standards Alignment

Grade Level	Common Core State Standards in ELA-Literacy
Grade 3	L.3.4 Determine or clarify the meaning of unknown and multiple-meaning word and phrases based on grade 3 reading and content, choosing flexibly from a range of strategies.
	L.3.5 Demonstrate understanding of figurative language, word relationships and nuances in word meanings.
	L.3.6 Acquire and use accurately grade-appropriate conversational, general academic, and domain-specific words and phrases, including those that signal spatial and temporal relationships (e.g., After dinner that night we went looking for them).
Grade 4	L.4.4 Determine or clarify the meaning of unknown and multiple-meaning words and phrases based on grade 4 reading and content, choosing flexibly from a range of strategies.
	L.4.5 Demonstrate understanding of figurative language, word relationships, and nuances in word meanings.
	L.4.6 Acquire and use accurately grade-appropriate general academic and domain-specific words and phrases, including those that signal precise actions, emotions, or states of being (e.g., quizzed, whined, stammered) and that are basic to a particular topic (e.g., wildlife, conservation, and endangered when discussing animal preservation).
Grade 5	L.5.4 Determine or clarify the meaning of unknown and multiple-meaning words and phrases based on grade 5 reading and content, choosing flexibly from a range of strategies.
	L.5.5 Demonstrate understanding of figurative language, word relationships, and nuances in word meanings.
	L.5.6 Acquire and use accurately grade-appropriate general academic and domain-specific words and phrases, including those that signal contrast, addition, and other logical relationships (e.g., however, although, nevertheless, similarly, moreover, in addition).
Grade 6	L.6.4 Determine or clarify the meaning of unknown and multiple-meaning words and phrases based on grade 6 reading and content, choosing flexibly from a range of strategies.
	L.6.5 Demonstrate understanding of figurative language, word relationships, and nuances in word meanings.
	L.6.6 Acquire and use accurately grade-appropriate general academic and domain-specific words and phrases; gather vocabulary knowledge when considering a word or phrase important to comprehension or expression.